I0471351

A GUIDE TO INTERNATIONAL OUTSOURCING

How to Achieve Success and Avoid
Common Mistakes

ALEXEY GODER

TATIANA GROMOVA

A Guide to International Outsourcing: How to Achieve Success and Avoid Common Mistakes / Alexey Goder and Tatiana Gromova,

Editor: Louis E. Tagliaferri

Illustrations by Sergei Korsun

Cover design by Svetlana Goder

The book is intended for mangers and engineers either involved in outsourcing or thinking about starting a project. The customer side managers will learn some tips how to make outsourcing successful while vendor side managers will get inside on the customer view of remote project management expectations. It will be interesting for outsourcing engineers to get clues about executive motivations of various management decisions. The authors hope that the book will make outsourcing more successful.

Copyright © 2013 Alexey Goder and Tatiana Gromova

All rights reserved.

ISBN: 1492835056
ISBN-13: 978-1492835059

DEDICATION

This book is dedicated to all our customers (past and present) – it has been our privilege to work with them.

CONTENTS

PREFACE

When we began getting involved in the outsourcing the whole idea of outsourcing was still new and few people have experience managing projects overseas. There was not much choice other than jump into a first project and start learning by experience. As a great surprise initial challenges arrived even before the first line of software code were written by overseas engineers. Now looking backwards from the top of our experience those challenges seem very expected. Solutions of the challenges had invented and the project got started. It was just a beginning of a long journey.

After years of managing projects we found ourselves answering a stream of questions how to do certain things in outsourcing. Over years as more new managers and engineers got involved in outsourcing and remote project management, they started looking for solutions to the similar issues we encountered before. Our colleagues and friends kept asking us again and again, so we decided to summarize our experience in a book. That's how this book got conceived.

We hope each reader will find something worthwhile to read in this book. There are a lot of publications with theory of outsourcing, however, you won't find much of the theoretical explanations hear, everything is based on our actual experience. Some readers may view the content of the book incomplete: we included everything we were asked or requested to explain regarding outsourcing, while other topics were omitted from the book. The content of the book was defined by the stream of questions we got to answer. If you don't find certain topics in this book, it means no one asked us about them. You may find some topic too obvious to write about again, but we have included it into the book because it was still something being unclear regarding the topic, and we were asked to give explanations about it. A historic perspective was included at the beginning of each section in order to present a broader view on the subject.

The book is intended for mangers and engineers on both sides: customer and vendor. The customer side managers will learn some tips how to make outsourcing successful while vendor side mangers will get inside on the customer view of remote project management expectations. It will be interesting for outsourcing engineers get clues about executive motivations of various management decisions. The authors hope that the book will make outsourcing more successful.

The following technique was used to write this book: the authors had been having weekly sessions talking to each other over Skype; the conversations were recorded and edited. These weekly sessions lasted over a year. Then the entire manuscript got polished. In some case we validated our ideas and tips by searching Internet. We used keeppy.com as a tool to capture and edit search results. Keeppy was very instrumental when preparing material for the book allowing multi-user editing in real time. The plan is to publish the book in English and Russian with some slight differences in the content: the Russian version includes more details about the employee compensation in the US while the English version talks more about paying employees in Russia. Also the section in English: "How to survive a business trip to Russia" is replaced with "How to survive a business trip to the US" in the Russian version.

CHAPTER 1

INTRODUCTION

According to Greek mythology, Zeus the king of the gods wanted to find a human capable of performing several complex assignments. However, it seems that no human was capable of rising to the task. It was out of the question, of course, for gods to intervene in affairs on earth. So, Zeus came down to earth pretending to be the husband of Alcmene, the beautiful daughter of Electryon and the wife of Amphitryon. Zeus mated with Alcmene who, in turn, conceived Hercules. Apparently it was all right for Zeus to get involved personally in this type of affair.

Hercules grew very strong and powerful. However, he was hated by

Hera, the wife of Zeus, who drove Hercules to perform terrible acts. At last repentant of what he had done, Hercules became subservient to King Eurysthesus, who he despised. King Eurystheus sent Hercules out on 10 assignments or exploits to atone for his actions. Hercules passed all ten of these exploits but King Eurystheus added two more because he considered one of the original ten to be performed in a somewhat unsatisfactory manner. Hercules completed the last two with success. The gods were happy with his overall performance and when he died he was granted immortality for his great works. In a way, this is an excellent example of outsourcing and how it works.

We use the term "outsourcing" to indicate that a business activity like manufacturing, product development, technical support or other corporate functions has been contracted out to another organization in geographic areas with less expensive labor. Usually outsourcing implies the placement of projects or production that occurs in another country. We will refer to a customer or a client as a company that contracts out its projects. Organizations that are commissioned by the customer that performs projects will be called a vendor or outsourcer.

Another term is "nearsourcing." This is used when projects are contracted out to be performed less expensively in certain areas of the same country or in neighboring countries with common borders. An example of this would be a USA company contracting out work to a company in Mexico so that the work could be done less expensively.

Sometimes a vendor contracts out a project or a part of a project that it received from a customer to a third party. If the third party is located in the same country where the project originated (the customer's country) then such a case is called "backsourcing." For example, a difficult part of a project may be "backsourced" by a vendor because the latter lacks expertise in a certain field.

1.1 History of Outsourcing

Outsourcing is a wide-spread economic phenomenon. It emerged in its modern form relatively recently when in the 1960s General Motors built a car manufacturing plant in Mexico. Why so late? The reason is that in order for outsourcing to be successful several very important conditions must exist.

First, it is essential for the emergence of outsourcing that industrially advanced countries reach a certain development level, since a company must have some technological advantage to justify moving its business activity to other geographical regions. In other words, there must be something to be outsourced. For example, from a historical perspective it is clear that Europe did not always have as technologically advanced state as certain other countries like China. In the middle of the 13th century, the Venetian merchant Marco Polo was engaged in industrial espionage in China. But, now things are different.

Second, there must be a sufficient gap in labor costs between countries or geographical locations for the outsourcing to be worth utilizing.

Third, developing countries must also achieve a certain level of professionalism; skilled personnel should be available, decent infrastructure should be in place, and reasonable security – both physical and intellectual (in order to prevent theft of intellectual property) should be implemented.

Fourth, it is necessary for the emergence of outsourcing to have a developed communications system, because without an effective operational link, remote management becomes unrealistic. By the mid-20th century a better developed telephone system emerged, airlines started to use jets for regular scheduled flights, and container shipping became a very cost effective way to transport goods. All of these advances have made it possible to move production or research to other countries.

Fifth, the political situation in the world should be relatively stable. Travel for business clients or freight shipping to another country must be safely accomplished. Look at the history of the early 20th century. Safety was out of the question for much of the period. World War I was followed by the Great Depression, much turmoil in Europe and in many other parts of the world and then World War II ensued. It was only sometime after World War II that all of the above mentioned conditions for outsourcing came to exist.

In 1960, for the first time in world history, General Motors established a precedent of outsourcing by assembling Chevrolet products in Mexico. Due to the differences in labor costs, the company profited. Following General Motors, other car manufactures erected assembly plants outside of the United States, but later returned because car assemblage became very much automated. Fewer workers were needed and the benefit of the wage difference diminished.

The next step in the development of outsourcing occurred in 1983, when an Indian company, Infosys, received a contract for the development of software from an American customer. Infosys had been created two years earlier, and this was its first experience in outsourcing. Infosys now thrives with approximately one hundred and thirty thousand employees.

In the 1980s some more outsourcing contracts were arranged, but these were still isolated cases. Explosive outsourcing growth occurred in the 1990s. This happened for two reasons: the invention of the Internet (and hence the possibility of rapid exchange of information by e-mail) and the decreased cost of telephone calls.

Outsourcing companies specializing in software development are for the most part located in India, where the prerequisites for such development are favorable. For example, among the developing countries, India is a political ally of the United States and Europe. Since India is a former British colony, there is a good system of education and a lot of English-speakers. Finally, India is a very large country, and it offers a lot of skilled personnel in the labor market.

China has established itself as a traditional place of industrial production, but it is less popular for software outsourcing. In many instances, Chinese companies take orders for software development and pass them on to outsourcing providers in India or Russia.

A number of outsourcing companies exist in Russia (however, there are relatively few) and in Eastern Europe (Belarus, Ukraine, Poland, Czech Republic). Other outsourcing locations include Hungary and Armenia in Europe and the Philippines, Thailand, Taiwan and Bangladesh in Southeast Asia.

1.2 Outsourcing Advantages

Business enterprises have always looked for competitive advantages, as seventeenth century English economist Adam Smith emphasized in his works. Outsourcing is just a modern tool with the same purpose – gaining competitive advantage. So, exactly how can outsourcing help businesses gain a competitive advantage? There are several ways this can be done:

Savings on the cost of labor. This ultimately lowers the product or service price.

Cost optimization. Businesses receive a degree of expense flexibility in their work. So, for a typical company, there are fixed costs (such as office rent, staff salary) and variable costs (e.g., consumable purchases). Reducing variable costs is pretty simple, while lowering fixed costs is a challenge. In a situation of a cyclic business, companies may be forced to lay off personnel due to a bad year, than hire employees again in a good year, then again lay them off in order to maintain the company's profitability. Outsourcing helps smooth out fluctuation in the overall headcount by moving the labor cost from the fixed expense category to the variable one. All the headache of laying off and rehiring employees is offloaded to the outsourcing provider. Large outsourcers may have more flexibility managing people. For example, they can reassign personnel on a project thereby reducing the number of employees per customer and increasing the number of staff members assigned to another project.

Optimization of financing. If the outsourcing provider is funded by venture capital, it is very profitable for the customer; certain expenses like the startup cost, office rental, recruitment, etc. fall on the shoulders of the investor. The customer pays only the labor cost for the work actually done in the outsourcing office.

Tax benefits. Sometimes when an outsourcing firm is used, the customer may get a tax credit. For example, Indian authorities willingly give several million dollars in tax credits to foreign corporations to stimulate job creation. When companies choose where to open new offices, Indian provinces compete with each other by granting tax credits. In Russia, an outsourcing provider with a certain number of employees may receive a reduction in social security and pension tax, and exclude value-added tax.

Optimizing efficiency. Minor and supporting roles in the production can be passed to the external side, allowing a company to focus on major issues.

Specialization of the staff. Savings on labor cost rates allow hiring more employees for the same amount of money. In this case, the company can fine-tune each team member's expertise and more accurately match the specialization of workers instead of using fewer, more expensive multi-talented employees.

Responsibility for the result. If a problem occurs during project execution due to error or negligence of its own staff members, the company would incur losses and have to deal with the consequences. In some cases all that the company could do is dismiss the responsible employees. In the case of outsourcing, the responsibility is also outsourced to the provider, which may be liable to the customer for the quality and timing of the deliverables. If the quality or terms are not complied with, the agreement between two parties may constitute some penalties to be applied to the outsourcer.

Environmental issues. This is a very controversial benefit of outsourcing. The environmental legislation is very strict in the United States and Europe. Moving environmentally sensitive projects to some other countries may result in cost saving due to more relaxed local limitations. Of course, no Western company would ever admit this and would argue that it strictly complies with all environmental laws, restrictions and requirements. However, the cost saving still occurs. The point is that it is the outsourcing provider (but not the customer) that must be in compliance with the restrictions and laws of the country where the projects are actually conducted. Local environmental restrictions in certain countries such as India and some countries in Southeast Asia are often less harsh than in Europe and the United States and compliance with those restrictions is becoming less costly. This item can also become one of the disadvantages of outsourcing, which will be discussed in the following section.

1.3 Outsourcing Disadvantages

Outsourcing can also have its disadvantages. Among the possible disadvantages are the following:

Remote management. The first and rather obvious disadvantage is that managing projects at a distance is more challenging than through local management. Sometimes it seems that the situation is black and white: either remote management is well established and the outsourcing works effectively or the management works poorly, projects fail, and the outsourcing ceases to exist. Unlike conventional management, in which there are also intermediate situations that you can work out and improve, outsourcing poses a very high risk of failure in the entire project if something goes wrong. Here is one typical example: a boss comes to an engineer and says: "You're doing a very good job, so we decided to entrust you with managing two more projects. But we know that you don't have time for it, so we will give you the assistance of two engineers from overseas." And the poor engineer, who has never engaged in project management or task distribution, says: "OK". There is a high likelihood in that case that the project will fail, because an outsourcing project cannot simply be arbitrarily assigned to an inexperienced staff or unit and then allows the remote team to fend for themselves.

Exchange of information. Although in the modern world, there are many means of long-distance communication, sharing information in different countries is not always easy. This problem is exacerbated by cultural differences of various countries. Ultimately, this affects performance.

Productivity of outsourcing is lower than if the work has been done locally. The time difference between continents further complicates the problem. In an outsourcing situation, the typical question and answer turn- around time is one day, as opposed to hours or minutes when all employees are local. Often for a quick completion of projects, engineers get invited to the customer's office for a few months, since the same employees work more efficiently in the local mode than overseas.

Developing a new product (from start-to-market) requires more time when using outsourcing, than the "classic" way of doing business. In addition to the above-mentioned productivity gap, the time it takes to finalize projects is affected by delays in the delivery and maintenance of parts and equipment necessary for development. Time spent on the logistics can be cumbersome. For example, Russian Customs can be a "black hole." The paperwork process can slow down significantly, meaning a delay of even months. If you are doing a project in China, and you need support for complex device manufacturing, the manufacturer may well say that you have to wait three months before his specialist can arrive to your location.

Information security. Outsourcing businesses generally are located in countries where intellectual property security is far from perfect. This leads to outsourcing companies becoming more vulnerable to information security than companies located in Europe and the United States.

The recruitment process is more complex. Often a manager decides on hiring as a result of an interview over the phone without a personal meeting. This is an additional risk. Sometimes a manager hires employees, works with them, and then dismisses them, never meeting in person – all just over the phone. There is no doubt that the required qualifications and experience of the manager would be higher in situations that did not involve outsourcing. It is more difficult to hire good, reliable outsourcing managers and in addition they cost more.

The governments of developed countries are not in favor of outsourcing (due to the already mentioned flow of jobs overseas). To date, companies have experienced no penalties (for example, in the form of increased taxes) for outsourcing. However, each new politician running for office in the United States makes promises to implement some penalties for losing jobs to business overseas.

The public opinion on outsourcing in the United States and Europe is rather negative because it is believed that local jobs are lost due to outsourcing. On the other hand, we are witnessing an increase in the overseas labor costs in the traditional fields of outsourcing which eventually will make outsourcing less attractive.

The climate inside the company. If the company actively uses outsourcing, its own employees start feeling less secure. People begin to think that their jobs may be replaced by workers overseas. This affects the morale climate in the company as employees feel uncertain about how long they can expect to work for that company.

Environmental problems occur, which we have already mentioned above, due to projects being relocated to countries with more relaxed environmental restrictions. This eventually causes additional damage to the environment.

1.4 Trend of Outsourcing

Outsourcing as a business has progressed past its initial development stage and is approaching a mature level. Although we have not conducted surveys or detailed research, we see several major trends in outsourcing based on our experience.

Companies are becoming increasingly virtual. Communication technology has developed to a level where employees no longer need to be physically present. As a result of globalization, large companies are dispersed throughout the world, including large outsourcing firms. International corporations have offices in many countries and their employees, working on the same project for several years, may never see each other personally. People get so accustomed to communicating at a distance that even employees located in the same office frequently use the same means of communication with each other as with remote employees. The notion of normal working hours is eroding. Managers require performance and on-time delivery, but not attendance. Over time, improved remote management mechanisms allow corporations to successfully operate on different continents and in different time zones.

Sometimes people apply the word "virtual" to businesses having a large portion of their business activity outsourced to various vendors. Speaking of terminology, to refer to a technical device we use the term "distributed system." Similarly, we would rather use the term "distributed corporation" or "distributed business" instead of "virtual corporation" or "virtual business" because the word "virtual" has a slightly different meaning.

Consolidation. The process of mergers and acquisitions of outsourcing companies will continue to form increasingly large players in the outsourcing market. This process creates new challenges for customers who are accustomed to dictating terms and conditions to their vendors. Now a large outsourcing corporation with hundreds of customers can tell each of them that each project is very small in volume relative to their entire business, and the vendor is in the position to dictate terms and conditions to the customers.

Environmental considerations. Many companies will become "greener," making their production more environmentally sound, using renewable energy sources like solar panels, etc. Outsourcing providers are following this trend in order to have one more reason to win a project in a competitive environment.

Nearsourcing is the latest trend of outsourcing in IT development in the United States. This means that a different source of labor in the same country, but different state, is utilized at a lower cost. Thus, although the jobs are created remotely, they still are not flowing outside of the country. However, in fairness it should be noted that this trend is rather artificial, created in order to prevent the disappearance of jobs within the country, and over time these jobs too will be outsourced.

Knowledge and expertise move from customers to outsourcers. Outsourcers keep gaining technology expertise and product knowledge from their customers. The center of gravity moves toward outsourcers, creating a potentially dangerous situation for customers' business. In a situation where an outsourcer managed to work for the same customer for a long period, the customer becomes a hostage of the outsourcer; it no longer will have the option to discontinue the business relationship and switch to a different provider.

1.5 The Four Most Important Things for Successful Outsourcing

Having examined the pros and cons of outsourcing and selecting potential vendors, you now decide to start the outsourcing project. Our experience suggests that there are several very important elements that are essential to the successful implementation of the project. These are *reporting, integration, feedback and information.*

Whenever insufficient attention is paid to any of these essential elements the risk of project failure is increased.

Reporting must be consistent and regular. We recommend using various means of reporting including teleconferences while strictly adhering to a set schedule. This will lead to disciplined and effective project execution.

The time differences between the client and outsourcing service provider add to the challenges. Some participants of the teleconference may be located outside the normal working time during conference calls. We recommend that the manager on the customer side agree to sacrifice his/her evening to hold a teleconference in the normal working hours of the performers. This will improve the effectiveness of the project as a whole, since it is difficult to schedule a group of people to gather at an inconvenient time, as opposed to one manager. If the conference call is scheduled outside of the normal business hours for the overseas team members, there is a good chance someone will be absent at each meeting. If the conference call is scheduled outside of manager's normal hours, it doesn't matter where the manager is physically located (behind the wheel, on a train, in office, or at home), the manager will be still able to call in and team performance will not usually be affected by that.

It is important that the conference is attended by all members of the group, rather than just a "speaker." The whole group should speak the language used for managing the project (usually English). It is considered a less effective practice to communicate through one person, who disseminates all information to the entire group. Inefficiency increases when a single "speaker" keeps track of all the information and spends the entire time talking to the team members and the customer. This person becomes a critical resource. If such a "speaker" decides to resign, then the whole project is in an extremely difficult situation, as it loses all communication and experience. This issue seems to be obvious, but unfortunately, such situations happen often in large companies.

Periodic reporting is a factor that contributes robust project execution. It is an easy mechanism to set short-term milestones and track progress. A typical reporting period is once a week. Besides progress reports, continuous exchange of emails should be encouraged. We recommend explaining to the members of the group that it is very important to take an initiative and send an email or call when an issue arises. If the manager is late with the next assignment for someone, the employee should write an email or call as opposed to sitting around and waiting for the manager to take the initiative. Sounds too obvious, so why do we mention this? Because it happens so frequently, even with employees of well-established outsourcing providers, we must emphasize it here. When the group enters into a rhythm and weekly conferences become common, members of the group may start to accumulate issues that they wish to discuss at the next conference. This causes a slowdown in the product development process, because instead of resolving the issue in a day or two through email, all issues are being discussed once a week, causing a delay in turnaround time. The manager should explain to the employees that work items must be resolved quickly, and they should react immediately.

Integration. It is recommended that the outsourcing unit be reasonably integrated into all business processes established by the customer. Integration starts with interviewing new candidates when hiring. We recommend that managers of the company-customer talk to each prospective newly hired team member. Then the customer will have a personal understanding about a new employee. Communication will no longer feel impersonal and faceless with remote individuals.

Document flow and decision-making procedures should be standardized with the procedure adopted at the customer site.

Meeting in person plays a critical role in outsourcing productivity. It is a good practice if all members of the outsourcing team travel to the customer site at least once to get acquainted with the culture in the customer's country, and it is even better to work in the customer's office for some time. When this is done efficiency dramatically increases, because the communication is entirely different after a trip. Imagine the following situation: a programmer from an outsourcing group has a question and emails one of the customer engineers. The engineer is surprised since he not only was unaware of the programmer's existence but also of the entire remote group's existence as well as the project that the group is working on. The engineer replies: "Why should I answer your questions?" A pointless conversation ensues that does not produce any results. When a programmer goes on a business trip and meets with all the engineers in person, then their communication process gets to a much more productive level.

At least once a year, the manager should attend a meeting at the remote group's site. It is difficult to overstate the importance of such a visit. Because the group is located at a distance from the customer, members often lose the feeling of usefulness. Interest must be maintained by keeping the performers informed of the results of completed projects. The manager will determine and explain the group's efficiency in this case.

Integration is much easier for beginners. They can more quickly become involved in the process and achieve maximum productivity.

Feedback. Without feedback, outsourcing will never be successful. It is necessary to constantly keep a finger on the pulse of the customer. We'll discuss some practical forms of feedback below. One of the most effective forms of feedback is periodic attestation by the client manager for each employee in the group. The system of monetary and non-monetary motivation for employees must be bound to this appraisal.

Information. When a group of engineers work in the same office over a complex high-tech project, information just hovers in the air, despite all the modern methods of communication. Because a remote group is not present they are denied this amazing ability to derive knowledge from those around them in the same manner.

The success of projects depends on the extent to which customer managers methodically bring information to the remote site, and performers can attain what they need to know.

1.6 What Does the Customer Expect from the Outsourcing Provider?

Imagine a competitive situation when there is one customer and several outsourcing providers. Which one gets the business? The winner will be the company that has a better understanding of the customer's expectations and has the capability to meet them. What are the most common customer expectations in the outsourcing business? Large established corporations may have different expectations and prioritize them differently then small startups.

Let's review both cases: large and small companies, starting from what is important for a well-established corporation when selecting an outsourcing vendor.

Intellectual property protection is the first priority. The customer should not have a slightest doubt about whether its intellectual property will be protected in the best possible way by the prospective outsourcing vendor. Otherwise the negotiations with the vendor will simply cease forever.

Business Reliability. This is the second priority: all aspects of the vendor business processes must be mature and trustworthy, because customers tend to opt for the long term business relationship. For a large company it is important to understand that the outsourcer will perform all the time and with the highest possible level of quality, ranging from direct work on projects to personnel management and equipment procurement.

Effective hiring. The third priority is that the outsourcing provider should be able to quickly hire qualified staff or locate employees within other departments and transition them from project to project. Not all needed specialists will necessarily be ready at the time of negotiations with the client. Outsourcing is a dynamic business; some projects move quickly, while others collapse. Different experts may be needed in the future on other types of work besides the initial project. This is why the ability to quickly hire professionals is more important than having all employees ready from day one.

Value. Finally, an important factor is the labor cost and related expenses. This may draw the attention of readers to question why money is only the fourth item in this list. Of course, cost is important, but if the three high priority items - IP protection, business reliability and effective hiring - are not satisfied, the outsourcing provider does not have a chance to win the business regardless how cheap it is.

Here is a different situation involving a small startup company that wants to develop a new product and bring it to the market. Note how the priorities are different.

The first priority is *the availability of highly qualified professionals* ready to start working on the project immediately. Future projects are less important. This is because the startup needs to develop a product and bring it to market as quickly as possible.

Time of completion of the project is the second priority. The customer will want to be sure that the outsourcer can perform the work not just fast, but faster than it would have been done without its assistance. If during the negotiation process it appears that this is not the case, the outsourcer losses its chance to get the business.

Value. The third priority is the cost, i.e. how much the customer can spend for project development. A large company is managing "budgets," while a startup is managing "money." This means that a large company may reallocate budgets and accept higher cost of the project if it is reasonably justified by the vendor. Of course it takes an effort on the vendor side to do so, but our experience shows this is not an uncommon situation. With a small company, however, the amount of money is so limited that talking about raising the cost of the project is pointless and will get you nowhere.

Protecting intellectual property. The fourth priority is intellectual property protection. Obviously, a startup must ensure that its ideas and trade secrets are not stolen, but in practice this issue is lower in priority than resource availability, development time and cost. From the first glance, this contradicts the importance of the IP protection for the startup trying to bring some new product to market. But it is a curious phenomenon that does happen. We are not ready to offer a theoretical explanation for the phenomenon, but it is based strictly on our experience. We encounter several cases when startup companies did not even bother to get a non-disclosure agreement signed while successfully completing high-tech outsourcing projects.

1.7 What Does the Outsourcing Provider Expect from the Customer?

Outsourcing providers have some expectations for their customers as well. If you do a search on the Internet for outsourcers having expectations for customers, you quickly find a paradox regardless how you formulate your search request. All search results will show the opposite i.e., what customers expect from outsourcing vendors— not what outsourcing vendors expect from customers. This means that the majority of related Internet publications discuss customer expectations (we talked in detail about this in the previous chapter) and ignore vendor expectations. However, it would be interesting to review what outsourcing vendors typically expect from their customers.

Specification. The first thing that an outsourcer expects from the customer is a specification, which is a document that details a step-by-step outline of what to do and how. Some outsourcers honestly believe that no project can be started without a specification. If there is a specification, then the outsourcer can estimate the time and cost of the project, if not, how can it be possible to enter into a commitment without such document? While it is generally a good practice to develop a specification and then start the project, surprisingly, many projects get started and are successfully completed not having specifications up front.   Developing a good specification is a separate project, and can be outsourced as well! The vendor may get a request to develop such a specification for itself. In practice, defining a project may come down to the customer saying to the outsourcer: "I have a client. Make sure that my client is happy!"

While working on one of the projects, one might face this situation: an engineering project was so vague that nobody in the outsourcing companies understood what to do. In one of such cases, the outsourcer started asking engineers from the customer company to provide them with project details. At first, no one was sufficiently knowledgeable to accomplish such a task, but then someone was found capable enough to start providing project details and specification. When the outsourcer got answers thoroughly and competently, the project was successfully implemented.   Only after that, everyone learned that the expert who consulted them was actually an employee of a competing outsourcing company and simply wasn't afraid to take responsibility and jump into the task preparing the specification.

Specification may be needed not only to facilitate project development. In Russia, in order to qualify for pension tax relief, a company may be required to supply a specification document to the Government tax authority (ignoring the fact that this is a trade secret). For such cases, companies sometime generate fake specifications without confidential information specifically for the tax authority.

Perfect business processes. There is a perception that if the customer is from the West then the customer's business processes are designed to be nearly perfect and that the customer's business operates effectively. The outsourcers believe that the customers' managers they will work with will do their part quickly and effectively. In practice this is not always the case. The reality is that in large corporations working relationships can be far from perfect and the amount of corporate bureaucracy and inefficiency can simply be too high.

New employees, coming to work for an outsourcing enterprise, generally think that their customers have a clearly organized structure, and that all projects will be super interesting. Actually, the work is not always effective, and the challenges faced are not always interesting enough or they are too routine. As practice shows, on average in outsourcing companies a person works for approximately five years. In five years the job becomes less interesting for the employee. This is one of the main causes of attrition.

Outsourcing to Western customers sometimes is wrongly assumed participating in the development of new "cool" staff while support looks boring and unattractive. New employees may get frustrated by the amount of actual support versus new development that he or she has to get involved in. We are aware of a case in which an employee resigned after a couple of months explaining that the reason for leaving was poor business process organization on the customer side.

Overseas employees often think that the customer has newer equipment than they do. In fact, the customer's equipment may be even worse than the outsourcer's. Upon visiting the United States, the outsource engineer might be surprised to find older computers and monitors in the customer's office than in his own office.

Feedback. As we mentioned above there can never be too much feedback! Outsourcers want to understand their customers, whether they are happy with the work or not, and if not, what the problems are and how they deal with them. Adequate feedback is a great quality for the customer to have! In practice, obtain as much feedback from the customer as possible.

Fast payment of invoices. Often the outsourcer expects that its invoices will be paid almost instantly, while the client usually has an accounting system of payment of, say, 30-60 days after billing invoice. In larger companies, accounting is setup in the way that expediting an invoice payment is close to impossible.

Independence. The outsourcer expects the customer not to interfere in the affairs of the vendor except for the project management and hiring decision making. While it might sound obvious that the customer should get involved as little as possible in vendor's payroll issues and the organization of work in the vendor's office, etc., our experience suggests that many US companies overdo micromanagement of these issues. Of course, ultimately, it all depends on the specific customer and its wishes.

CHAPTER 2

INTELLECTUAL PROPERTY PROTECTION

2.1 Dual-Use Technology

Dual-use technology commonly refers to those technologies that have been developed for military purposes, but are used for manufacturing civil products and visa-versa technologies developed by non-military applications and later used for military purposes. The main issue with the dual-use technologies is that often you cannot avoid using something that might also have other military application while manufacturing a non-military product.   Some very peaceful products may require dual-use technology for their production. And the products may be quite simple and commonplace. For example, dual-use technologies are used in the manufacturing of microprocessors, computers and even light-emitting diodes for general lighting.

Governments strictly control dual-use technology proliferation by defining and maintaining lists of which technologies are permitted for exportation. Accordingly, if an overseas outsourcer works with some dual-use technology, time and effort is spent to obtain government licenses.

In Russia the media often uses the term "dual-use technology" to refer to the following kind of situation: a plant produces defense products and additionally has developed production capability for certain civilian products during a difficult financial period. These products might include saucepans, washing machines, etc. The plant then uses its ability and equipment to produce the civilian products, and, in fact, no military technology is used for production. As an example, the plant "Hydromash" (Nizhniy Novgorod, Russia), which specializes in gear for military aircrafts, in "the hungry years" also manufactured washing machines, canning and beverage seam devices. The term dual-use technology" should not be applied to such cases.

2.2 History of Dual-Use Technology Export Control or Why There Are No Cuban Cigars in the United States

The history of this seems to begin in the year 1917. Apparently, the first government trade restrictions on something military related, while not considered a weapon, was the Trading with the Enemy Act passed by the United States Congress.

As we said, "dual use" means that somehow, even indirectly, the technology is related to the "war" as well as to civilian use. Mankind has been conducting wars since pre-historic time, and has invented, manufactured, and sold weapons since then. However, Government restrictions to limit the trade in arms and military technology emerged only recently on the scale of history. One of the first documented cases of public restriction on arms sales was the Hague Conference of 1890 that dealt with the issue of slavery in the world and banned the sale of weapons to countries where slavery still remained. But this directly restrained trade.

In 1914, the United Kingdom adopted the Trading with the Enemy Act, and subsequently repealed it. This legislation was associated with the outbreak of the World War I and prohibited any trade and commercial transactions with companies or persons considered "hostile." This included all military and non-military products, even annual payments on earlier commitments, as well as payments of dividends to shareholders, if any were considered to have hostile connections. In 1916, a court trial took place between two companies, Daimler and Continental Tire and Rubber. The latter company was not paid for the supply of car tires to Daimler, because all except one of the shares of Continental Tire and Rubber were held by residents of Germany and all directors were German residents.   Daimler was concerned that payment might contravene the 1914 Trading with the Enemy Act and other common law issues. First the Court agreed that at the time of the transaction the provider was not hostile in nature. However, the High Court decided that the provider may become hostile in the future, and the payment for already supplied tires was against the Trading with the Enemy Act.

At the beginning of the World War I, the United States confirmed its neutrality and continued to trade without restrictions. And only three years later when the United States decided to join the war, its government formed a similar law. And if the English Act of 1914 prohibited absolutely all trade with enemies, the history of selective trade restrictions began in 1917 with the United States Trade with Enemy Act. Strangely enough, this has nothing to do with the socialist revolution in Russia. So, the Congress of the United States, on October 6, 1917 gave the President the power to restrict the sale of exported goods if they might fall into the hands of the enemy. Prior to that, the President did not have such power. For modern readers it seems odd that the President of any country may not have such power and could not deny trading of something. But then, at the beginning of 20th century in America, what prevailed was not the word of the head of State, but the notion of private property. The disposition of property at its owner discretion was a sacred human right. Trading with enemies was an issue of the property owner's relationship with God or with his or her own conscience and allegiance to the State had nothing to do with it. Therefore, the introduction of even a small restriction of that right was an important historic moment.

But, back to the year 1917. The President of the United States had the right to determine the categories of products and to limit their exports in case these products might benefit the enemy, just the same way the English law was set in the Trading with the Enemy Act. The law could be applied not only weapons, but also to any other goods, with potential connection to the war. However, this right of the President was not permanent, but only applicable in a time of war. The declaration of the beginning of a war and its end was an exclusive right of the US Congress. This was the first time in history that the spread of sensitive technologies was limited. Being provoked, the United States decided to join the World War I on the Triple Entente side, which was the first US intervention in the war in Europe. Among other actions in preparation for the military campaign, the Trading with the Enemy Act was adopted.

Interestingly, the Act does not extend to citizens of the United States, that is, if for some reason a German soldier was a citizen of America, he could buy anything from merchants in his homeland, and United States President had no right to prohibit him. After the end of the World War I the President's authority to restrict the trade ceased.

In 1933, Congress expanded the powers of the President of the United States. Now the head of State could restrict the export of any goods not only in a time of war, but in emergency situations. Martial law would be imposed by the Congress, and the decision of whether a situation is an emergency would be made by the President himself, so this was a significant increase in governmental power. Franklin D. Roosevelt, who was President at the time, once received these rights to combat the Great Depression. He announced a state of emergency and for five days closed all banks. It is believed that this dramatically affected all economic processes and after that America began to recover from the Great Depression.

The presidential power to restrict trade was unsuccessfully challenged in court several times. In all cases the courts sided with the Government.

In 1977, the presidential power to restrict trade was changed by the US Congress. Now the President cannot impose new restrictions but can only reconfirm previously existed ones on the annual basis. Once lifted, a restriction can no longer be imposed again by the President. Some trading bans were ceased, but the Cuban embargo survived. The President still had the right to cancel the old injunction; however, all Presidents of the United States including Barack Obama, have reconfirmed the Cuban embargo. Therefore, there are no Cuban cigars or Cuban rum in America.

So, can everyone except for the Cubans, relax, live quietly, and trade freely? No, new mechanisms to monitor dual-use technologies have been implemented. The reason came at the beginning of the cold war. In Western Europe the Marshall plan — assistance programs for victims of the World War II — was being implemented. The USSR refused to take part in the Marshall plan, although its participation was originally envisaged. The USSR instead independently developed technology and later joined the Warsaw Pact. Political relations intensified, and as a consequence, in 1949 at the initiative of France, the Coordinating Committee for Export Control (COCOM) was established. The Committee was composed of NATO countries and some others. The goal of the Committee was to monitor the spread of weapons and dual-use technology. The headquarters were located in a wing of the United States Embassy in Paris.

Countries in the Committee, were not bound by a treaty which formed the basis of the work of the Committee, they were only able to adopt their own internal laws restricting dissemination of dual-use technology. However, each country had the right to a veto. If a country member of the Committee decided to sell any dual-use technology in the Socialist bloc, and its own laws allowed it, any other Member of the Committee could impose a veto. In that case the country member merchant was expected to comply and to cancel the shipment.

European countries considered this right as a way to delay the technological development of the USSR and the Socialist bloc. It was assumed by European countries that the delay should be for five years. In order to achieve a delay of five years, each year 20% of the items from the list of prohibited technologies would have to be reviewed and then labeled as unlicensed sales. Accordingly, new technologies were added to the list. The United States regarded the veto as a tool for political pressure i.e., if the USSR behaved badly then punish it with another veto! Of course, technology companies lobbied their Governments to ease export restrictions because the market in the USSR was significantly undeveloped.

World War II did stimulate technological advance in the USSR. But then, probably due to export restrictions, the USSR and the countries of the socialist camp came to be considered behind the West technologically. COCOM lasted a little over 40 years. The cause of its collapse was a change in the political situation associated with the collapse of the USSR.

2.3 Definition of the Export from the United States

Anyone involved in outsourcing (regardless whether their role is employer or worker) faces the issue of export. There are export laws, common to many States, but each country also has its own existing laws. In this chapter we'll talk about the features of the US export laws and licensing of export operations.

In the United States export is regulated by the Bureau of Industry and Security at the Department of Commerce. The main export regulatory document is the Export Administration Regulations. Most technologies and products do not require export licenses. Documents published on the website of the Bureau determine the list of products and technology with military or dual-use. The Bureau also defines the rules for classification and the obtainment of export licenses.

So according to modern American law, exportation is not a right but a privilege. This privilege may be restricted or taken away by the government. On its website, the Bureau publishes blacklists of individuals and organizations that are prohibited from export operations.

The export operation is, firstly, moving anything outside the United States, regardless of whether it is manufactured initially in the United States or not. For example, the return of previously imported goods after a technical exhibition into the country of the producer is considered an export operation. It turns out that the manufacturer can bring their device to an exhibition in the United States, but returning it may require an export license, if the device is connected with dual-use technologies. The license, of course, can be obtained, but the device will remain in the United States, while in waiting for the license approval.

Technology, information, software, etc. are also objects that can be exported. They obey the same law: if American technology is being sold somewhere abroad this is also considered an export operation. Remotely accessing software located on a server in the United States is an export transaction as well.

Technology information transferred electronically to outside of the United States is also considered an export, including the return of previously imported information from other countries to the United States. Of course, it does not make sense returning back an electronic copy of the data. However, if the data has been changed within the US before returning this information it gets the status of U.S. origin i.e., partially manufactured in United States, and then returning the modified information to the country originally importing it from the United States will be deemed an export.

Secondly, American laws define the transfer of ownership of anything manufactured in the United States that occurs outside the country as an export transaction. For example, a computer manufactured in the US that is physically located in Europe and that is being sold to Russia, is considered by American law to be an export.

Thirdly, products manufactured outside the United States using technology created in the United States, or the components produced in the United States, are also seen as exports and may require a license to sell to a third country. The need to license in this case depends on the percentage of American parts that require licenses, and the country of destination.

Finally, there is the concept of the "deemed export," which is a technology transfer to a person who is not a citizen of the United States, including those living in the United States territories. By the way, the United States is the only country that sees this as an export. If a foreign specialist gets hired by a US company to work on a project related to dual-use technologies, an export license is required!

An export license is not needed if the foreign employee acquires the right to permanent residency in the United States (with a "Green Card") or even American citizenship. In this case, the transfer of information ceases to be an act of exportation. But until then the employer must apply and get the license granted before the project start.

Giving a speech at a conference before an international audience is an act of exportation. A fairly common situation is when some conference presentations are touching topics related to dual-use technologies. In this case, the conference organizer must submit in advance who their listeners are, and take care of export licenses.

Violators of the export laws in the United States face four types of punishment:

1. The ban on export for a certain period;
2. A fine (numbered in tens of thousands of dollars) for every minor violation;
3. A fine of five times the volume of illicit export or in the amount of one million dollars, whichever is more, in the case of serious violations;
4. Ten years of imprisonment

Violation of export laws has occurred with even the most well-known of companies. IBM once was fined for 8.5 million dollars for exporting to Russia without an export license. Compaq received a fine of 2 million dollars. Sun Microsystems was punished by the prohibition of exports for the year. A person, named Charlie Kwan from Northern California, received ten years in prison and a fine of 250 thousand dollars because his firm had hired three Chinese citizens. The Chinese worked with instruments classified as dual-use technology, without a license. Kwan had applied for the license, but was refused. He decided to risk it anyway ... but at a great price.

Recently there have been other similar cases. It was "found" by an internal audit at Meritor, Inc (former ArvinMeritor) that in 2005 and 2006 the company supplied its products and technical data in a number of countries, including China, without getting a proper export license. The issue was caught in 2011, and the company voluntarily informed the Bureau of Industry and Security. The Bureau fined the company for 100 thousand dollars and has published on its website that it applauds the integrity of the company. In another case, TW Metals, Inc. was fined at 575 thousand dollars for violations of the supply of titanium and aluminum alloys in China and Israel in 2004-2007.

2.4 What We Sell

Some products and services require an export license. So, how do you know which products require a license and which do not? This issue is clarified by U.S. federal regulations that specify which products require a license from the Department of Commerce. First, however, exporters must determine whether their product or service fits within the Export Control Classification Number (ECCN) system. This classification code consists of five alpha-numeric characters that identify the technology level, product or service capabilities, country destination, customer and intended use of the export.

The First Character: Digits 0-9 represent the category within which the product or service falls. The most problematic code is 0 which is associated with nuclear materials. Telecommunications and information security are indicated by the digit 5.

The Second Character: Products or services are arranged within each category by groups. These are Group A – Equipment, Assemblies and Components, Group B – Test, Inspection and Production Equipment, Group C – Materials, Group D – Software and Group E – Technology.

The Last Three Characters: These provide detail about the reasons for the control of the technology or product.

The result of this classification system is that there are long lists that indicate which activities require an export license. By the way, if it is not possible to classify a particular technology then it gets the code EAR99, meaning "everything else." An export license in this case is not needed unless it is intended to be delivered to a country for which there is an embargo.

If a company is not able to classify their activities independently it may hire an external consulting firm to assist it.

The classification of exported technology can be quite challenging. It is recommended that you call the Department of Commerce if you have any questions about export classification. For example, an export license is required for certain types of dual-use technologies and for working drawings of the source code of software. On the other hand, supporting documentation can be transmitted without a license. But, as mentioned above, a foreign export license is required for the development of such software programs. In the process of doing so, programmers create supporting documentation related to changes made in one or another version of the program. This supporting documentation includes snippets of source code software. The question is whether the license for the transfer of documentation, including fragments of the original text, to persons who are not citizens or permanent residents of the United States requires a license. This question was asked of the Department of Commerce and, contrary to expectations, it responded that a license is not required.

In unclear cases the U.S. Department of Commerce gives permission for access to technology without a license more often than one might think. It should be noted that the decision is given within the context of the license application, including the history of intellectual property rights in the company, the absence of denials of export licenses and the nature of dual-use technology. Outside the context of this approach, the determination of the appropriate license may be different.

For those of our readers who have now decided that the U.S, export laws are too complicated, we can give one example of Russian export control laws that are required in order to import goods into Russia with the consent of the manufacturer. That is, if someone decides to import honestly something that he bought during a trip to the United States (an iPhone, for example) then he needs permission from Apple, the manufacturer. It is clear that this law is applied very selectively and individuals act on it rarely. However, for commercial businesses it is a cause of premature graying of hair on the heads of managers.

2.5 Software Exports from the U.S.

It is important for IT companies to know that the transfer of computer software, or remote access by persons who are not citizens or permanent residents of the United States, is an act of export, regardless whether the recipients are located outside or inside the United States. In the case of dual-use technology, an export license may be required depending on the location of the recipient company and the nationality and residency of the persons receiving access to the exported software. For example, a license is not required if a U.S. citizen is sent on an assignment to Russia and takes a laptop with dual-use technological information. However, a license may be required if the "subject" wanted to remain in Moscow to live there permanently and continue to work on a project, exchanging information with its headquarters in the United States. A Russian export license may be needed for this case as well. Later we will explain the procedure for obtaining a Russian Export License. By the way, let us note that the above example is based on real events, although it seems speculative.

Software source code and executables are classified differently, even if the software associated with the technology of dual-use pre-compiled executables can in many cases be passed without a license. If the source code of the program is laid out for open access, regardless whether it is associated with the dual-use technology or not, an export license for transmission is not needed. That is, if the company has managed to post a full source code of the program on its web site, then from this point on an export license is not needed. Another issue is why the company disclosed its trade secrets and whether this was done correctly. If not, then perhaps after posting the code that the company will not need to export (no matter that there may be other licenses) and after a long and thoughtful dialogue with representatives of the law, the firm might simply cease to exist.

Because of the need to license anything related to dual-use technologies, there is a mass of ambiguous, complex situations. For example, a firm in the United States buys a program developed in China and by any criteria it becomes clear that this program must be licensed as dual-use technology. If the buyer finds and fixes errors in the program then it cannot send the corrected version back to China without obtaining an export license because it now becomes an exportable program that is used in the development of dual-use technology.

Software usually is developed as several modules or components. This allows separate modules of the same package to be classified differently in order to determine the need for export licenses. Imagine that a process plant consists of various technological components and is running software consisting of separate components. It might be that some of the technological components are classified as dual-use technology while others are for "peaceful" purposes. This is possible, for example, in the semiconductor industry in the production of microprocessors. Each component is running a software module. But, there are universal modules serving all of the components (for example, the user interface). The software modules that are designed exclusively for the components of dual-use technology require export licenses in order to be transferred from the United States, while the universal modules for management and certain other components do not require a license. Such an approach permits the outsourcer to develop modules that are not export controlled and that do not require a license. Often management tries to obtain a license that covers the broadest possible area of the software in order to avoid future questions. We recommend that you call the Department of Commerce and get feedback directly from them. The Department of Commerce usually supports a differentiated approach to export classification and, in some areas, allows a less restrictive approach.

In America there are export restrictions on software that contain encoding information. Therefore, U.S. exports to Russia, such as a firewall where the encoding is used, an export license might be required. The Bureau of Industry and Security regularly reviews security licensing requirements in order to facilitate export. The last such revision was in June, 2012. We recommend that you consult with the Bureau's website for the latest changes in requirements.

2.6 Who We Sell to

Returning to the U.S. export laws, in addition to what is to be exported it is important to obtain an export license, determine to whom the goods, service or information will be sold (important with respect to the country and to the profile of the company and customer), and determine how the goods will be used by the buyer. For example, if we want to export pens from the U.S., how they will be used by the customer is important. It is all right if you write a book about outsourcing but if the purpose is to use the pens to draw blueprints of nuclear bombs then the pens cannot be exported.

There are "black lists" of individuals, companies and countries that are prohibited from exporting anything without a license, even if it is humanitarian aid. The countries on the "black list" are Syria, Sudan, North Korea, Cuba and Iran. In other countries there are less stringent restrictions imposed including China, Russia and the former Soviet republics, which are not EU members. In the former republics that do not have nuclear weapons, the restrictions that are imposed are more lenient than for Russia.

If the purchasing firm is associated with military production or research in nuclear physics or weapons of mass destruction then the seller of the product will need an export license. However, the license will not usually be given.

The buyer of dual-use technologies is obligated to the preservation of the dual-use technology and its use for peaceful purposes. The seller is obliged to ensure that the buyer is able to fulfill these obligations. In order to obtain an export license both the Seller and Buyer are jointly responsible for developing a "Technology Transfer Security Plan" that is a comprehensive document that should be filed with the Department of Commerce. The exporter, in this case, has the responsibility to check on how the plan is being executed for some time after the export operation. In addition, U.S. consulates have a designated employee who is responsible to monitor compliance with dual-use technologies. These officials may conduct verification audits.

2.7 How to Obtain an Export License in the USA

As we have said, the responsibility to obtain export licenses in the United States rests with the exporter. Some exporters sell without a license. Then Government officials come into their office and see well educated people in suits and begin asking tough questions. Often they make an innocent expression on their faces and say something like "Oh my god, we did not know that we needed a license." That does not work. Remember the dramatic fate of Charlie Kwan who was put away for ten years for not observing U.S. export controls. We do know that some companies have exported goods to Russia without a license due to ignorance. Fortunately, the export license in those cases happened to be unnecessary.

So, having decided to work with someone abroad, a company must find its classification of export controls based on the principles of classification that we discussed in the previous chapter. In the table published by the Department of Commerce you must find your classification number and determine whether or not you need to request a license for this kind of activity. If the table does not provide the answer then you should hire an outside consultant or call the Department of Commerce to learn if a license is needed. If a license is needed then it is necessary to prepare the proper documents for a license application.

The Department of Commerce requires that you provide information about the future buyer. The exporter must determine whether the buyer will trigger "red flags," which are suspicious circumstances that might become an obstacle to obtaining an export license. A "red flag" by itself is not a reason why the license application may be denied; it only serves as a cause for further investigation. Here are some examples of "red flags."

• The firm is on a "black list" and has already been refused a license for a serious reason.

• The address matches the address of an importer company that has already been refused a license or the receipt of goods or it is close to that address (same city and street and the address number differs only with respect to an office or suite number).

• The buyer does not want to give full information about who is the ultimate customer.

• The buyer wants to acquire technology or a high tech device but its technical capabilities as the user are not consistent with the technology. For example, a "red flag" would be triggered if a small private bakery wanted to buy a super complicated and expensive computer.

• The technology or the high tech device does not meet the technological level of the buyer's country. For example, a firm wants to buy semiconductor equipment in a country where that industry basically does not exist. Another example would be if a firm wants to buy a machine for the production of microprocessors but there is no application for the technology where the machine would be used i.e. why do you need a motor but not the whole car?

• The buyer wants everything at one time and has no interest in installment payments, credit, etc.

• The company has just been established and little is known about it.

• The buyer waives the seller's equipment installation, user training and consulting support.

• The date of delivery to the buyer is uncertain.

• The purchase is made at the point of delivery – far from the point of end use.

• Delivery is ordered to the office of the carrier (from which point it is clear that the product will be further shipped, but that explains why the seller does not immediately order delivery to the end point).

• (An explanation must be made regarding the point of delivery. Take a common situation where the customer is a U.S. company and the outsourcer is Russian. In order for the Russian firm to produce the goods it requires some equipment that must be provided by the customer. In order to avoid dealing with Russian Customs, delivery of the goods is ordered for any place, but not in Russia. However, it should be clear that in this case the contracting firm is at risk of losing not only the export license but also of getting a fine or a more serious punishment.)

• The buyer is not able to answer whether he would use the products domestically, or resell it to another country.

• The product is ordered in a strange configuration or package. For example, the purchased equipment is for the manufacturer of microprocessors but it is ordered without a device that performs a key function.

If "red flags" exist, then the firm applying for an export license must write to the Department of Commerce to explain and justify the situation and why it should not preclude the Department from issuing the license that has been requested.

A petition for an export license must be accompanied by information about the export product. Here is what applies to these informal documents:

Description of Dual-Use Technologies that will be exported. This document need not be extensive; it is just a summary of the activities of the manufacturer and the purchaser, a description of the technology and the components it uses, including software. When compiling this document you should focus on those points that require the license rather than try to write everything at one time. It is necessary to accurately describe exactly what will be sent. Particular attention should be placed on intellectual property; describe what the transferred source is, the software, user manuals, drawings, samples, etc. For example, the method of transfer of goods in electronic form through coded channels between two firewalls. You must indicate how the intellectual property will be protected by the recipient. In order to do this, refer to the separate document "Security Plan for Technology Transfer," that regulates the procedure for the protection of intellectual property.

Security Plan for Technology Transfer (technology transfer security plan). This is a very important document that must be approved by both the exporter and the importer and that is usually signed by a company official. The plan defines the nature of the business relationship between the exporter and the importer (seller-buyer, customer-outsourcer, etc.). The document identifies those persons who are responsible for the implementation of the plan (Export Compliance Officers) both for the exporter and the importer, the procedures that will be followed and how the staff is recruited. The plan might specify, for example, that each new employee hired by the outsourcer must be interviewed by a representative of the customer company, that a background investigation must be made and that personnel files must be collected. It might describe how access to the premises of the outsourcing operation can be gained i.e. the use of electronic badges and visitor rules. An important and extensive part of the plan is the security of electronic information.

The plan uses the principle of "need to know" where access to information is granted only to those who directly work on the project. It spells out the fact that each employee must have a password to access a computer and it denies access if a certain time in the workplace is exceeded by time locking the computer's screen. More specifically, the password can be a code issued by an electronic device that looks like a key ring. The code changes every minute.

The document also stipulates how information is transmitted between the customer and the outsourcer. It states which members of the staff shall have the right to copy information to removable media (for example, to work at home) and on what terms and conditions may they be permitted to do this. It also sets forth the procedures for training new staff and for periodic staff retraining. Part of the plan is an agreement on confidentiality: what information cannot be disclosed to employees and for how long a period of time and who is responsible for any violations of the agreement. As a general rule, the person who discloses information about dual-use technology is subject to immediate dismissal and is subject to further liabilities including criminal prosecution. Note that in the Russian Federation it is difficult to prosecute for the disclosure of such information. But if the person comes to the United States he will be arrested very quickly. Also spelled out in the terms is whether the customer must verify the safety of outsourcing and how often it will perform the inspections.

The basis for the construction of the document is the requirements of the country that wants to protect the spread of dual-use technologies. In turn, the customer company wants to protect its business information. The requirement of the country and of the companies might not be the same, but the plan must satisfy both parties.

In addition to the two above-mentioned documents, the Department of Commerce may request other detailed material related to the technology or products to be exported. It can, for example, require all engineering documentation, all specifications, instructions and drawings.

Note that all documents for an export license in the U.S. are provided in electronic form. The license, itself, is just a letter that is sent as an e-mail. There are no paper or hard copy documents that are signed and sealed. The e-mail letter simply gives a license number, expiration date and the terms of export.

Typically, the procedure for obtaining the export license takes about three months. A month is spent on the preparation of the initial set of documents. Upon receipt of a petition for a license, the Department must provide a response within 30 days. Usually, after the initial filing there are questions that we must answer. Then we wait and if we are lucky the license arrives. The license is not unconditional. A typical export license limits the type of technology transfer method and stipulates that everything must be in compliance with the security plan for the transfer of technology. Typically, the export license is issued for two years, it can then be extended. The probability that the Department of Commerce will deny a license is not great. But, instead of refusing it can tighten the list of conditions that must be complied with by the exporter and the importer.

The Department of Commerce's jurisdiction does not apply to certain special cases such as exports of nuclear materials or animals. However, these areas are outside the scope of this book. For our purposes, the criteria for a license by the Department of Commerce will suffice.

2.8 From Russia with Love. Exports from Russia

After the collapse of the Soviet Union into separate states the first attempt to control the spread of dual-use technologies can be considered as the decree of President Boris Yeltsin (11.04.92 N 388) "On measures to establish a system of export control in Russia." At this time COCOM was living out its last moments and the Wassenaar Arrangement did not yet exist. The decree did not set out a list of dual-use technologies, but rather only required one to be developed. Subsequently, the decree was repealed and replaced by other legislation.

Exports from Russia are defined by the law of 1999 and in addition there are some Decrees of the President of the Russian Federation and other normative documents. An export is defined as the movement of something from the customs territory of the Russian Federation to beyond its limits, including re-exports of previous imports. This definition also applies to the transfer of information abroad, presentations at foreign conferences, etc. The disclosure of information to foreign persons in the Russian Federation is not considered an export and is not licensed. In general, export restrictions in Russia are easier than in the U.S., but the procedures for obtaining licenses are more difficult.

At the time of this writing, the current list of dual-use technologies established by the President is dated December 4, 2008.

There are two organizations that control exports: the Export Control Commission of the Russian Federation and the Federal Service for Technical and Export Control (FSTEC). The boundary between these services is blurred, some saying that the federal service issues export licenses for exported technology or dual-use goods. The Commission for Export Control authorizes private entities to carry out an independent examination of export credentials.

The system of export controls in the Russian Federation is focused more on the Russian side (whether the Russian company is registered, what its relationship with the Internal Revenue Service is, etc.), while in similar cases US authorities focus on the foreign recipient it is important to know who gets the goods or technology and how to control the use of technology. Its duties include FSTEC formation of "black lists" of unreliable companies, but these lists are not published.

If an organization wants to engage in exporting it should first read the information on the superbly organized FSTEC site. And while the FSTEC website is well organized, the Government exporting rules are complicated and confusing.

As in the U.S., it is the duty of the exporter to make a classification of exported goods, technology and information. In Russia, this classification is called identification expertise. The exporter is entitled to be a self-identification expert, but it can also refer to the special expertise of another organization. A list of accredited expert organizations can be found at FSTEC. In practice, exporters always refer to such organizations in order to absolve themselves of responsibility.

If the examination has determined that this type of technology is controlled, you have to get permission to export it through one of the following documents:

General license issued by the determination of the Government of the Russian Federation for exports to certain countries. General licenses do not apply to the export of technology. In order to obtain a general license an exporter is required to have an internal export control program. Such a program must be confirmed by the Government before applying for a license.

A Single license issued by FSTEC for the one-time export of goods or technology. The license term is for a maximum of one year.

An export permit issued by the Commission on Export Controls for the temporary export of goods and technology followed by a return, for example in order to demonstrate at an exhibition.

Obtaining a license may not actually be sufficient for export. The fact is that Customs in the Russian Federation does not report to FSTEC and does not recognize licenses issued by the FSTEC as being a sufficient basis for export. Customs may decide to require an additional determination that the dual-use exported goods cannot be attributed to military products. Such determination might be reached by an expert in the Department of the Supply of Arms and Military Equipment at the Ministry of Defense. The question then arises as to who has the authority to issue export documents to begin with? For that answer let us quote information of the FSTEC site that states: "Experience shows that there is no universal answer to this question. It is advisable that organizations that often export or import products in a certain range, agree with Customs on a list of findings for customs purposes and try to resolve these issues (with the Russian Defense Ministry, Federal Technical Committee of Russia, etc.) in advance of the submission of the cargo customs declaration (CCD) document, "The process of making decisions on the licensing of…" on website http://www.fstec.ru.

If the result of the examination of the identification findings was such that an export license is not needed, Customs might still request confirmation of these conclusions from FSTEC and the Ministry of Defense. This problem disappears in the case of exports of electronic information technology because Customs is not involved in the process of direct exports.

2.9 How to Get a One-Time Export License in the Russian Federation

For a single export license you first need to find a customer to produce a product or do a project. You must then enter into a contract with the customer before you can apply for an examination and obtain a license. FSTEC sets forth a procedure for applying for an opinion regarding the need for a license without actually issuing the license, itself. However, even this process requires the delivery of a contract.

The next step is identification expertise. As we mentioned, the services of expert firms provide almost everything. These organizations require the customer to provide a number of documents. The first is the matter of shipping documents that reflect the nature of the foreign trade transaction, in other words the contract between the exporter and the importer. Also required is the technical documentation for the products such as certificates of product quality, data sheets, etc. If the exports are subject to scientific information or advice, you should provide information about the method, location and time of information transfer. For the examination you will be asked to provide originals of drawings and prints that are identical to those that will be exported. Therefore, if someone is doing a review for western customers, the written report of the review must first be given to the experts and then to customers. In a situation where the export is a presentation at a foreign conference the information provided would be about the conference.

The experts performing the examination are required to maintain trade secrets and not disclose information that they acquire.

The result of the examination is the classification code TN VED that determines whether an export license is needed. Note that unlike the situation in the U.S., the determination of whether or not a license is needed does not depend on the recipient's (the importer's) country.

When the examination of credentials is completed you can begin applying for a license. The FSTEC website shows a complete list of documents that must be provided in order to obtain a license. In all you will need about 12 documents. The exact number varies depending on the situation. All documents must be provided in paper form and documents of several pages should be printed front and back and then stitched or glues together. All copies of the documents must be notarized. Upon receipt and verification of the documents, FSTEC will conduct its own examination, which is recognized by the provisions of the Government.

In order to check who will become involved in using the exported goods or technology produced in Russia, the authority requires that the documents filed for the export license application are accompanied by a contract between the exporter and the importer. In some cases a document from the importer is required to guarantee that the use of the product or technology is for stated purposes and not for otherwise and that it will not be re-exported. In other cases, when a product or technology being exported is somehow military related, the declaration of the importer must be confirmed by competent state authorities of the importing country. FSTEC requires that you provide a "document of the authorized state body of the country controlling end-use products, confirming the commitment of the foreign recipient (the end user) regarding the use of the derived products." This requirement is due to the fact that in Russia there is a procedure for obtaining the so-called "import certificates" and there is state control over the use of imported goods and technology for declared purposes. Because the U.S. does not have anything like this, this requirement brings the importer to a dead end where, for example, regarding an American company that wants to purchase Russian dual-use technology, it is not clear whether the U.S. entity will be in a position to confirm that it is a private company and that it will fully comply with all of the requirements imposed by the Russian state agency charged with monitoring the activities of the company. If private companies transfer the acquired technology to someone else in violation of U.S. export laws and regulations, then sanctions will follow against the company by the U.S. government. As we saw above, very respectable companies can be fined huge amounts of money e.g. IBM. If an American company is using imported technology within the country then the US Government requirements have been satisfied even if the contract between the importer and exporter is breached. In contrast with the Russian Federation, public authorities do not provide control over the transfer and use of imported technology within the country, and therefore cannot guarantee the good conduct of the importer if the technology stays within the US borders.

Consider this hypothetical example: A domestic U.C. importer sold dual-technology obtained from abroad. The buyer was a US company working in the military field and intends to use the acquired technology for military purposes. We will also assume that the company is properly licensed for the manufacture of military products. In this case, the importer might have breached its contractual obligation with the exporter who is the manufacturer of the dual-use technology, but it most likely did not violate any rules of the U.S. Government. The exporter has an option to challenge the importer in the court, if an audit shows an improper use of the received technology. But, this can be done only after the fact of the contract violation. No Government authority can guarantee before the export transaction occurs that the importer will behave well! Only God can guarantee this, but the Russian export authority still requires a guarantee document!

How is this situation resolved in actual practice? As an example, an outsourcer tries to request state guaranteed documents from U.S. customers, but the clients do not provide the documents because they do not know where to obtain them and thus they use their own letter as a guarantee document. In such cases, FSTEC takes such letters and issues licenses without the official state documents. By the way, in a similar situation with respect to obtaining an export license from the U.S. to Russia, supporting documents from the Russian government is not needed, although such documents may be issued by FSTEC.

The decision to grant a license takes 45 days. If the decision is positive, then a license must be issued within three days after it is made. The license is a piece of paper with seals and signatures. There is a procedure that must be followed in the event that you lose that sheet of paper. Outsourcers hope that the transition of government services of the Russian Federation to an electronic document management system (which now appears to be an American luxury) will enable the petitioner to send all documents by e-mail and to receive a license also by e-mail.

Under the export regulations, the export license issued in Russia for the one-time export of exports is for a fixed period, usually one year. The exporter is required to report the execution of the license to the Federal Technical Committee. The license expiration must be reported within 15 days after expiration and must be accompanied by a report with supporting customs documentation.

The Federal Service for Technical Export Control inspects organizations that have been issued export licenses, whether or not the export operation takes place and will notify company about the inspection in advance. On the FSTEC website future inspections are listed several months in advance.

2.10 Software Exports from Russia

Unfortunately, in the Russian Federation it is very difficult to carry out the procedure for obtaining an export license for software being developed in the field of dual-use technologies. The law permits the export of intellectual property including software. However, the licensing procedure is set up to export tangibles, but it is not suitable for the participation of Russian outsourcers in the development of dual-use technologies.

One of the main obstacles is that you must have a completed product before obtaining a license. Strictly speaking, FSTEC does not require this specifying only the following wording "materials that reveal the nature and content of technology" in the list of required documents. However, all expert organizations and government officials have interpreted this requirement as meaning that there is a need to provide the full source code and all technical documentation concerning it in the completed form. The development of complex software systems for a foreign client requires frequent (usually daily) synchronization of the intermediate versions of the developed source code with the server of the customer who is abroad. The following will help explain the development process. Let's suppose that a group of programmers based in Russia require constant communication with the customer. It will be necessary to jointly develop specifications based on the requirements of the customer, perform coding, testing and integration with the customer in order to correct errors in the software and prepare documentation. The rule is that if the testing takes place using the customer's equipment, then at every step you must perform a regular synchronization of information between the participating employees and customer. At each step there is the synchronization of information in electronic form from the Russian Federation, i.e. the act of exporting does not fit into the existing scheme since an export license would be needed before beginning work. The same problem arises with research activities; it is required that you provide a complete report at the beginning of the process of applying for a license. There is no mechanism by which the customer can legally send intermediate results.

This problem is also exacerbated by the fact that one-time licenses are issued only for a single act of exports that is ready to transfer the software code for one time. Sending the corrected version technically requires a new license. Multiple licenses for the export of information in Russia do not exist. FSTEC does not issue multiple licenses and general licenses issued by the Government are not subject to the export of intellectual property.

On top of all that, export licenses that are issued for only one type of product are defined by the classification code TN VED. This might create another problem. Imagine that the exporter has developed a software package for managing a complex technological setting associated with several different technologies that have different codes. In Russia there is no procedure for obtaining a license for multiple codes. A procedure for obtaining multiple licenses for the export operation is also one that does not exist. So, it is hoped that an expert organization will classify the packet to only one code.

An outsourcing company that produces software can bypass the problem of obtaining a license as follows: all programs, documents and other information should be located on servers overseas and programmers should have only remote access to the servers. All work should be done on those servers and the code should never cross the border of the Russian Federation in any way. Intellectual property should always remain with the client and the entire project should look like a "virtual rendering of services without the export of intellectual property."

The Russian government could easily solve these procedural problems without any significant costs. It would require only a few things:

• Allow FSTEC to issue export licenses for certain a duration and for a certain importer allowing multiple export transactions of the same nature under the license.

• Obligate FSTEC to apply to the Ministry of Defense, if necessary, to get military use expertise for the technology being exported

• Eliminate the requirement to provide complete source code for software projects or reports in finished form for scientific research. Instead, require only "materials that reveal the nature and content of technology" exactly as stated in the FSTEC requirements.

• Ensure that the Russian Customs Service does not require any additional documents other than the FSTEC license.

2.11 Import of Dual-Use Technologies in Russia

The import of dual-use technologies is controlled by the Government regulation "On the verification of compliance with safeguard obligations of imported and exported goods and services of dual-use in the stated purposes," as amended on February 4, 2005. This ruling directly states its purpose, which is "to prevent the unauthorized re-export from the Russian Federation goods and services of dual-use previously imported to the Russian Federation with the guarantee of declared purposes." It determines the requirements of obligatory registration for Russian organizations and enterprises regarding the use of goods and services of dual-use according to stated purposes of state control over their performance and it also monitors the obligations of foreign importers regarding the safeguard of goods of dual-use that are acquired in the Russian Federation. The regulation provides the procedure for obtaining an import certificate for the imported goods or dual-use technology. The regulation gives FSTEC authority to issue such certificates "if the public authorities of the exporting country require the provision of such documents." For example, the U.S. does not require providing certificates and in the case of exports from the U.S., and such certificate would not be necessary. In practice, Russian Customs always requires certificates regardless of the exporting country requirements.

The regulation defines the procedure for obtaining permits in the event that the importer wants to transfer (sell) the imported technology to other companies within the Russian Federation. In that case you need to send a request to FSTEC, together with the application of contracts and other documents, and then wait for 15 days. As a courtesy to the manufacturer, the Russian Government checks on whether the exporter agrees to the transfer. A similar practice does not exist in the U.S.

The same regulation defines the procedure for an audit to be made to determine compliance with the stated objectives of importing technology. Inspections are carried out with respect to both Russian and foreign companies exporting from Russia. FSTEC is authorized to check Russian importers. The same procedure defines the process of the foreign company audit. A special commission must be formed to conduct the audit. Officials of the manufacturer, the Ministry of Foreign Economic Relations, the Ministry of Foreign Affairs, the Federal Customs Service and the FSB must be represented. The regulation is formulated so that the Russian exporter is not allowed to conduct the audit by itself, only the above commission can do so. However, there are no known cases in which Russian private (non-Government) companies have ever tried to audit the foreign importers for the proper use of technology imported from Russia.

2.12 Intellectual Property: What it is, Why it is Necessary to Protect it and How to Do it

2.12.1 "Rule of the Calf" in the History of Intellectual Property

The history of intellectual property protection is as old as the history of mankind.   Rock carvings dating to the 5th millennium BC have been discovered in the caves of Lascaux in Southern France. In the caves are images of bison with marked characters that presumably identified the artist who made the drawings.

In ancient Egypt and Mesopotamia (3500 BC) stone carvers made an identifying mark on the blocks that they produced and in many countries of the ancient world potters branded the pots that they made.

In the year 500 BC in the Greek city of Sybaris (now located in present-day Italy) there was an annual cooking competition. The contest was won by the person who produced the tastiest dish and that person was awarded exclusive rights to produce that dish for a period of one year. The word "sybarite" is derived from Sybaris because the residents of that wealthy city led an idle and effeminate way of life.

The first serious issue of the protection of intellectual property arose in China during the Tang Dynasty (7th Century BC). The issue concerned the replication of the technology of copying prints on textiles and leather - paper had not yet been invented – and dealt with the matter of copyright control.

In Ireland the first lawsuit for copyright protection was filed during the 6th century. The case involved an accusation of plagiarism by St. Finnian of Moville against a former student of his, St. Columba, both monks. Finnian was the owner of a translation of the bible that he had brought back to Ireland from Rome. Columba decided to copy the original so that he could help spread Christianity throughout the world. Finnian protested Columba's action as infringing on his rights. The two monks agreed to arbitrate the matter before Diarmaid, the High King of Ireland, who was the supreme judicial authority. The king made an historic decision by stating that "As to every Cow its Calf, so to every Book its Copy." In that time if a calf wandered away from its owners land into someone else's property it had been the practice for the owner of the other property to try to claim ownership of the calf. But, the law on that matter ruled that the calf belonged to whoever owned the cow. Thus, Diarmaid ruled that the copy belonged to the owner of the original.

It is believed that the first patent was issued in 1331 by England's King Edward III of Flanders to John Kempe. The purpose of this act was to attract foreign artisans to England and to promote the use of English in the industry. It is not known whether John Kempe was the inventor of anything new, so the document issued by King Edward III may have been more like what we call a license in the modern world.

In the 15th century Venice was the equivalent of the Italian version of the "Silicon Valley" – a center of technology. The first patent law was developed at that time in order to consolidate the rights of inventors of the technology of glass production. Before that, an inventor had to go to court to prove the right to an invention after the "know how" of the invention had been stolen by someone. For the first time, the Venice law introduced the registration of inventions and guaranteed those rights to the inventor for a period of 10 years, protecting the inventor from future encroachments of the invention.

In 1710 Britain passed a law on copyrights, protecting those rights for 14 years, renewable for another 14 years.

In 1771, for the first time, Russia abolished the state monopoly of the printing press and in 1783 it allowed private printers. Later, the Society of Russian writers and playwrights became engaged in copyright protection. After the Russian revolution, only four days after the capture of the Winter Palace, a decree, "On the State Publishing House," was issued that defined the right of the state monopoly on printing for a period of five years.

In 1928 the Soviet Union passed a law that recognized the copyright of the author for life and for 15 years for his or her heirs. Gradually this law was extended. Current copyright laws vary from country to country and are very complex. But, in many cases the rights belong to the author for life and then to the author's family for up to 70 years.

But since then, laws to protect intellectual property against theft have been developed. One of the most extensive attempts to commit industrial espionage in the history of mankind was the attempt to ferret out the secret of making Chinese porcelain. Chinese porcelain first appeared in Europe in the 12th to 13th centuries AD, but the method of manufacture was not known. In the 12th century Marco Polo brought many Chinese inventions back to Europe, however the secret of how porcelain is made was not among them. The Europeans were apparently not able to steal the secrets of the original Chinese process but they kept trying anyway. In one such attempt a stolen Chinese porcelain formula was misinterpreted and the production of high quality bone china began. At that time bone china was unknown in China.

The attempted thefts continued until the beginning of the 18th century when in 1708 in the city of Meissen, alchemist Johann Friedrich Böttger and scientist Ehrenfried Walther Von Tschirnhaus discovered the secret of hard porcelain.

Even before these events, the tradition of having tea had already appeared in England. But, imported porcelain was very expensive and very fragile and it was prone to crack with hot liquid. Therefore, it was the practice to first pour in a cup or cold milk and then to add hot tea. As a result, to drink tea with milk became a national practice, but that tradition was later happily forgotten.

2.13 What is Intellectual Property?

Intellectual property usually refers to creations of the mind. In a narrow sense, intellectual property is something that is protected at the state level. In a broader sense it is any information that gives an advantage to those who use it.

There are for types of intellectual property rights that are protected by the state.
1.   Patents
2.   Trademarks
3.   Copyright
4.   Trade secret

Of course, there are other types of intellectual property that can be described as being "unprotected by the state." For example, a designer comes up with something brilliant. His idea is also intellectual property but the state does not protect it because it is not clear how to do so. But, the designer can obtain a patent for his idea, in which case the intellectual property will be of a different type.

Now, consider the four "official" types of intellectual property rights in detail.

2.13.1 Patents

A patent grants the right to use intellectual property for one's own use and is recorded by a government body. Typically, a patent is issued for something physical, something that can be touched. But, there are exceptions. During the early to mid-1980s there was an argument as to whether patent law could be applied to software or not. Now software can be patented and that kind of patent is considered valid. Under that patent the owner can transfer the right of use to another party for a fee. In the U.S. patents are valid for 20 years. Note that there is cost to owing and maintain a patent, i.e. the patent holder must pay for the registration of patent rights and during the term of the patent must constantly pay to maintain it. If the patent is not maintained then the right to the exclusive use of this type of intellectual property is lost.

In both Europe and the United Stated patented information, itself, is not a secret. The word "patent" is derived from the Latin verb "pateo" that means "to open, to make available." There are websites that have a shared database of patents with a full description of what is patented. This enables someone to read what the patent is but they cannot use it. Frequently, patents are subjects to dispute but in order to avoid lengthy and costly litigation, the disputing parties may agree to settle the matter amicably. Note, that it is difficult to win a patent court suit because the matter of patent law in the field of hi-tech requires complex technological expertise.

The patent is limited to the country that grants it, that is if the patent was obtained in America it solely applies in the United States.

Patent law is different in different countries. The U.S., Europe and Japan have agreed on a system among themselves. But, there are serious differences among other countries. For example, in the United States the pharmaceutical company Pfizer has not been able to patent Viagra because in 1994 the patent was filed simultaneously in the U.S., Europe and in China. Because the patent application is public information, Chinese pharmaceutical companies have now mastered the production of such drugs. The patent laws of China permit a challenge to the legality of issuance of a patent once it has been confirmed by the state. In 2001, Pfizer's patent for Viagra was challenged in Chinese courts and revoked because the original application was not sufficiently detailed. Pfizer appealed to the Chinese courts, arguing the claim that the rules regarding registration applications were changed between 1994 and 2001 and when it was originally filed in 1994 the original application was adequate. The governments of the United States and of European countries have put pressure on China to conform the Chinese patent system to the requirements of the World Trade Organization (WTO) of which China is a member. In 2007 the Court of Beijing restored the rights of Pfizer to Viagra.

Here is a situation that illustrates the conflict situation in the field of patent law. Imagine that a major American or European company that manufactures high-tech devices like cell phones or computers has intellectual property including patents on the products that it wants to sell in Russia. In turn, Russian companies have a right to their patents. A potential problem exists in that the ideas protected by Russian patents can be used to manufacture these products (the cell phones or computers). Theoretically, the owner of these patents can apply to take a foreign company to court, but it is always a resource intensive process for anyone to sue. This involves the need to carry out complex and costly investigations and to pay for the work of lawyers.

In practice, the situation is resolved like this. Some organization buys patent rights from the patent owners in a certain country and area. They then sell them "wholesale" to the manufacturing company of the high-tech goods. In the end everyone is happy. The manufacturer of cell phones or computers can work quietly, without distractions and the need to go to court is eliminated. The original owner of the Russian patent received a certain amount of money and the proxy company received its share of the profits.

2.13.2 Trademarks

A brand can be a name, phrase or symbol that is associates with a product or service. In Russia the terms trademark and trade name are used interchangeably. A trademark can be registered in the U.S. for a period of 10 years and is renewable for an unlimited number of times. However, in the U.S. a trademark registration is not required. It is sufficient that the owner of the brand or trademark declare it as such, for example by posting it on its website, and inserting the symbol "TM" next to it. However, registration of a trademark is necessary in the event that there is a challenge to the trademark that must be litigated in court. In Russia, on the contrary, the right to a trademark is established only after official registration.

2.13.3 Copyright

The purpose of a copyright in the United States and in Russia is to protect a form of expressing an idea, but not the idea itself. For example, in the case of a literary work, a copyright protects the form of presentation of the novel, but not the story plot or idea. It would not be permissible to publish a novel like "Romeo and Juliet," change only the cover by putting on your name and then claiming the work as your own. However, a copyright would not prevent you from retelling the story about the two lovers, Romeo and Juliet, in your own words and publishing that work.

In the case of software copyrights, the algorithm cannot be registered. However, you can write a program and it will be subject to copyright.

Typically, copyright arises from the creation of intellectual property – the author can somehow copy its offspring. As with trademarks, in the U.S. it is not necessary to register a copyright. Unpublished original works are protected by common law copyright. Published original works are protected by copyright when the author associates the proper copyright indicia with the published work. However, as with trademarks the formal registration of a copyright is necessary in the event of litigation over the published work. In Russia, in contrast to the law regarding trademarks, it is not necessary to register a copyright in order for it to be valid.

2.13.4 Trade Secret

A trade secret is any information that gives the owner an advantage. There is a close relationship between the definition of trade secrets and of intellectual property, but the important difference between a trade secret and the three previous types of intellectual property is that a trade secret must be kept confidential by its nature. Historically, in the United States, the laws regarding protection of trade secrets vary among the various states. There are two elements that are required in order to establish a violation of a trade secret:

• The information that potentially might be stolen provides some advantage technologically or with respect to the act of doing business.
• Substantial measures have been taken to protect the trade secrets.

For purposes of explanation, you cannot set up a website, share certain information and then say "This is my trade secret." A classic example of a trade secret is the recipe for Coca-Cola, which has been carefully safeguarded for many years. As required by law, all of the ingredients are listed on the packaging of the beverage. The percentage and proportion of ingredients used in the production of Coca-Cola, however, are unknown. There have been many unsuccessful attempts over the years to accuse Coca-Cola that some ingredient is being withheld from the labeling.

2.14 Why Protect Intellectual Property?

Many companies carefully safeguard intellectual property because it represents something of great value to them. The loss of intellectual property would be especially critical for pharmaceutical companies because although the production of drugs may not be difficult, the process of creating new drugs is extremely resource-intensive. A similar situation exists with software; development is complex but production is less so.

There are also cases just the opposite, where development is very simple but production is very difficult. One example is that the processing of making wine itself is relatively simple. However, to precisely replicate a particular wine is extremely difficult because due to various environmental conditions, grapes grown on even adjacent fields will often give the wine a slightly different taste.

In the United States we can say that the protection of intellectual property is at a paranoid level. The reason is first that if intellectual property is leaked in any form it is almost impossible to stop the leak. Secondly, it is extremely difficult to bring the "spy" to justice and punishment.   Quite often the issue does not concern documents or drawings but rather oral information passed over the telephone. Trying to prove who said what to whom is very difficult.

If someone steals diamonds and they are recovered they can be brought back to the owner. But when information is disclosed the damage can be long lasting or even irreparable. At the same time many companies are trying to figure out what their competitors are doing; which means that there are entire businesses engaged in the gathering of 'Intelligence." For example, often people who work for a competing company will pose as "head hunters" or employment agency staff. They invite employees of the competing company to interviews where the real purpose is to try to ferret out trade secrets. Someone may be called by a person posing as the staff of an imaginary head hunter. The person might directly say, "We are looking for a specialist in a certain area. Who are you? Are you the person we are looking for?" But, more subtly, the supposed head hunter, having made a list of employees of the competing firm, contacts the right person and asks, "We are looking for specialists who are versed in such and such technology. Do you know anyone we could contact?" About half the people bite at this bait and say, "Oh, yeah, I'm an expert." And thus they wind up sharing trade secrets. Often a competitor does not necessarily know the specific technical information desired, but enough so that a general direction toward it can be developed.

Another method of industrial espionage is the tracking of publications. For example, if a group of students has published several articles in a particular area and then has ceased to publish anything this would be an indication that the group may have been hired by a firm that is interested in developments in that area. A more serious indication would be if students from different universities who are working on a problem no longer publish articles on that subject and even move into the same place suggesting that they have been hired.

There once was a story about a situation that took place in Australia. A certain enterprising company decided to sue a large American company claiming that the latter violated its patent rights and used elements of the invention of the Australian company in its products. In order to prove the allegation they hired a professional spy. When the spy received the assignment, he began to study what products of the American company could potentially use the disputed technology. Next, the spy studied a forum where users discussed products and what worked, what did not work and what was being worked on but still had bugs. After this the spy signed up for training classes provided by the manufacturer, where he got a lot of details about the firm's products. The spy and a lawyer summarized this information, made a claim and file a lawsuit. The trial lasted for some time, but eventually the American company paid a decent amount to the Australians. Incidentally, the spy's fee was a quarter of a million dollars.

Another example is of a company that manufactured high-tech equipment that, from time-to-time, broke due to software errors. Technical support programmers looked for what failed and the clients sent in complete log files of user actions. Thus, the programmers in this case became very knowledgeable about the processes used by the customers and could convert what they learned into solutions that were later provided to other clients. So, by eliminating the problem for one client, the programmers unknowingly gave out trade secrets to other clients.

Here is a more concrete example of this situation. A company manufactures equipment for a certain technological process that involves rapid heating. One of their customers successfully used this equipment for ultra-fast heating and has improved the process by making certain adjustments to the software settings. The manufacturer was not aware that this could be done. However, in connection with the information obtained about a technical support request, the programmers of the manufacturer were surprised to learn that the customer was using the equipment in an unintended way. But, after a while another customer asked the manufacturer's programmers if it were possible for the equipment to heat faster. The programmers said that it was possible and gave the customer all of the parameters that in general were actually trade secrets of the first customer.

In order for IT staffs to avoid inadvertently giving away trade secrets they should be given special training. This also applies to those departments like design engineering that directly interface with a customer in the process of providing technical support.

2.15 Ways to Protect Intellectual Property

In the West, violators of intellectual property law are held accountable by penalties that range from fines to time in prison. In Russia it is rare that cases of this type are prosecuted.

In the U.S., on the other hand, the paranoia is so high that people are afraid to violate someone else's rights in this area. For example, if any company somehow acquires a document that indicates it is the intellectual property of another company, the document is immediately returned to the owner with the assurances that no one has read it. If this is not done and the facts emerge, then it is likely that a lawsuit is inevitable. One sensational case involved a Chinese outsourcer of Microsoft that used stolen software. Microsoft did not know this and included it in its product. The company that was the copyright owner learned about this and sued Microsoft. Of course, Microsoft survived financially but the outsourcer that allowed the use of someone else's code lost all of its customers.

For any company, the protection of intellectual property is, in fact, just like any other business project. There are two categories of security requirements; the first is when a firm is trying to protect its trade secrets and the second is when the government imposes certain standards of protection regarding military technology, dual-use technology and other important secrets. The requirements of these two categories do not always coincide, but the company must be able to find a compromise.

Companies define security requirements with respect to exactly what they want to protect and how to do it. For example, we have already mentioned that in the medical (pharmaceutical) field "secrecy" is very strictly enforced.

Much has been published concerning the protection of intellectual property. Here we are only touching on key aspects of this problem. Each company builds a defense system that consists of two parts: physical protection (physical security) and the protection of information (information security). They prepare documents that spell out the nature of the organization's technology and also a list of types of information that should be protected such as e-mail, drawings, source code, software and so on. There is information that is not confidential and this will often be found on the company's website for public access.

It is important to determine how to restrict information access by the company's staff. As we have already mentioned, this is most often done on the basis of "need to know" information that is only available to those employees who need it to work on a project, etc. As a general rule, the entire system uses passwords for access to information, as well as the use of electronic keys (small devices that display frequently changed codes). In order to gain access to certain information a user must enter both a password and the electronic key code.

Employees are trained and coached in information security. Each participant in the business process is explained in detail why it is important to protect intellectual property and what the responsibilities are for the maintenance of privacy. However, sometimes incidents happen. In one company the IT employees of one department wrote an article for a conference that referred to the operations of another department. The information was not released, but the fact that even within one company people learned about the work of another department caused a serious situation.

Particular attention is given to the training process to ensure that an employee does not even unintentionally release trade secrets to another customer.

Typically, companies require non-disclosure agreements to be signed by their suppliers, customers, employees and visitors that specify the nature of the information that should not be disclosed, the terms of the agreement and the persons on both sides who are bound by it. Often, this is a one-sided document that applies only to information received by the signatory. For example, employees of Facebook at its Menlo Park Campus are allowed to invite visitors just for lunch (lunch is free for employees and visitors), but even visitors must sign a confidentiality agreement. The text of the agreement depends on whether the visitor has come on business or just to eat. If the person just dines, the document is signed only once. If over time a visitor is hungry again, then it is not necessary to sign another document. The text is likely the same no matter whether the visitor came for breakfast, lunch or dinner.

For physical security, there is a system of badges for entry and exit in the different segments of the firm's premises and there are rules of access for employees and visitors to the premises with restrictions for the use of mobile phones that are integrated with cameras, etc. In addition, there are rules governing the sending and receipt of goods and parcels. Security requirements also dictate how the evacuation of the premises should be made in the event of a fire threat. There have been times when the fire alarm triggered and the staff rushed to evacuate according to the procedures, but that left empty offices that could have facilitated the entry of outside parties who would have had access to trade secrets.

The last thing that we want to say in this chapter is that companies should regularly conduct internal audits to ensure compliance with both physical and information security requirements. We have already mentioned examples of U.S. Companies that have voluntarily informed the State retrospectively about export law and regulation issues.

2.16 Specificity of Protecting Intellectual Property by Outsourcing Companies

The outsourcer must be able to organize its work so as to meet the requirements for protecting the intellectual property of all of its customers, which, in turn, might be working with several outsourcers. At the same time, customers can be from different countries and the governments of these countries may have their own rules with respect to maintaining control over export information in the case of dual-use technologies. In addition, the outsourcer might have its own requirements for the protection of intellectual property. All of these requirements have to be met at the same time

One issue is the flow of information from one customer to another, which should not occur through the staff of an outsourcing organization. If a customer wants to inspect the work of an outsourcer, it must be ensured that no information beyond the scope of the inspection was accessed. The solution to this problem is the physical separation of employees. Each employee should work for only one customer. Accordingly, outsourcing staff that work for different customers should sit in different rooms and their access badges should not open someone else's door.

It is not always possible to comply with the rule that "one employee works only for a single customer." When you need the services of specialists in very narrow fields of physics or chemistry, it may simply be that the number of experts available is less that the number of customers and the fact must be accepted that any one specialist might have to work on the projects of competing customers. Here is an example, an American company hired a Russian outsourcing firm in the field of LEDs and requested that the outsourcing firm sign a standard document that stated it (the customer) had the right to conduct inspections at the developer's representatives and that the customer had the right to access computer data. The outsourcer refused to sign the document on the basis that they kept information about other customers on the same computers and their auditor's office would not allow the customer access to those computers. The customer considered this and agreed that in this case the outsourcer's refusal was justified. The project, nonetheless, was successfully completed.

If a customer wants to begin working on a project with an outsourcer, it is important to understand how the system of laws and the judicial system in the country of the outsourcer operate. In particular, if we are talking about India, China or Russia, the general recommendation is to hire an outsourcer that has substantial property or funds in the client country. Why do this? Suppose that a customer has major claims against an outsourcer and the court within the country in which the outsourcer is located is asked to resolve the claims. If the outsourcer has no property in the country of the customer it is not at risk. The judicial system in Russia does not work the best way. Things are slightly better in China and India. When recruiting an outsourcer, the contract should stipulate that any disputes will be arbitrated in the country of the customer. Tripartite agreements between the client, contractor and third party should also be used to ensure that the outsourcer will effectively protect intellectual property. The third party to the contract must also have property or funds in a country where the judicial system works effectively, such as in Europe or the United States. In such cases, if the outsourcer "misbehaves," it runs the risk of its assets being attached in a lawsuit.

As we have mentioned, there are cases where the customer does not enter into a written contract with the outsourcer to perform work but issues only a purchase order. After all of the above, it seems like this would be contrary to common sense and would be impossible. The reason why a customer may not care about this is very simple; the technology is so specific and so unique that it is not of interest to anyone else. If this is not the case, then it is important that a well-constructed contract be drawn between the customer and the outsourcer. The contract should clearly spell out who owns the intellectual property created in the process of outsourcing. Incidentally, this point often is a stumbling block in negotiations between potential customers and outsourcers. Thus, in the Russian Federation, universities and scientists often believe that the intellectual property and anything else that they come up with belongs to them and to no one else. But, the customer wants to own everything that relates to the intellectual property process. In order to prevent disputes, the customer might want to see the employment contracts that have been prepared between the outsourcer and its employees to learn if they provide for who owns the intellectual property that is created. The customer might also want to verify the documents signed by each employee concerning the non-disclosure of inside information and determine how they were made and whether everything in them is true. This policy should especially be done in situations where an employee is transferred from one project to another being done for a different customer. In such cases, the employee should be precluded from working on information for a new customer that is the intellectual property of the first customer. The employment contract should prescribe limits like six months, a year or two years from the time of termination until the employee is allowed to work for a competitor.

Texts of agreements must be translated into the language of the country of the outsourcer. Often, contracts that are written in the language of another country are considered void. In particular, this applies to the Russian Federation.

It is useful to have documents that describe what kind of work is done for the client by the outsourcer. For example, each employee should have a notebook or document in which he records what he did including such information as what was done to resolve a work issue, what was discussed at a meeting on a certain date, etc. The document may be, in particular, multiple files on the employee's computer. The documents would be required to prove if the employee of the firm, say, Ivanov, did indeed perform certain work and if the firm, in turn, used the work of Ivanov in the project being performed for the client company. In the event of a lawsuit, this information could be required to prove patent rights.

Sometimes it takes a lot of time getting such documents, but it is absolutely necessary. Sometimes the actual work takes up a negligible amount of time while the main effort is on various types of coordination. For example, one firm produced gas analyzers for medical devices. In order to make changes to the software source code it was necessary to carry out a complex, multi-step approval procedure. That took a lot of time, but it was justified by the specificity of the development of the medical devices.

It is often necessary to conduct special training in order to motivate employees to maintain the proper documentation. This is more important for Russian engineers than for their U.S. counterparts due to the cultural differences. Even if the American does not understand the validity of any claims, he will still do what he is told. If the Russian does not know why, he will not do it (or if he does, it will turn out badly).

Here is an example; a lawsuit in the field of patent law is filed. The customer argues that he acted on behalf of the development outsourcer but in order to prove this, it is necessary to provide documentation. It turns out that the outsourcer changed the name of its company so that in the course of the project it would receive tax credits from the state. In order to make this a reality, the firm had to either change the name of the company, or separate it into several units that were then united together. As a result, it received a decision that the project was carried out by members of a company that was different from the one that was awarded the original contract by the client. Consequently, because of seemingly insignificant name changes, the customer suffered huge damages – much more than would have occurred if the project was done by its own employees rather than having placed it with the outsourcer.

2.16.1 Protection of Electronic Information in Outsourcing

In order to achieve more effective protection of intellectual property, outsourcers often disable the USB ports of computers and disconnect access to the Internet, except through the company intranet system that allows only a limited amount of email with attachments so as to prevent the mass mailing of designs or software codes. Security personnel can at any time see what an employee is doing on his computer.

2.16.2 Physical Security in Outsourcing

Outsourcers restrict access to their offices through the use of electronic badges. Often, an employee of one department cannot gain access to a different department where the employees are working on projects for a different customer. In situations where there is an open space office layout, department separation can be accomplished by setting up cubicles that are partitioned with opaque glass. In every department the printer can be loaded with paper of a different color: yellow, blue, green, etc. When an employee checks out of an office, the security staff checks to see whether he has a document printed on colored paper with him.

Outsourcers often control the use of mobile phones, especially those with a built-in camera. It is usually strictly forbidden to photograph displays. Visitors' cell phones may be subject to confiscation.

The customer may request that a specific access protocol be followed by the outsourcer. The standard procedure is that all visitors must be accompanied by a member of the staff.

In America there is a common requirement that the guards for the security staff of a company not be employees of the company. The customer may request that the guards not be employees of the outsourcer.

2.17 How to Successfully Pass an Audit

Traditionally, in Russia the word "audit" refers to the verification of various documents of private enterprises that is conducted by some state agencies (e.g. tax authorities). Also, a company may order an internal audit in order to detect errors, for example, in its own documentation. However, the outsourcing business has another concept of the meaning of an audit – one that involves checking on the work process by the customer.

When and how an audit will be conducted is agreed in the contract between the customer and the performer of the work. An audit might vary in the degree of its depth and comprehensiveness. The most extensive audit is one in which the representative of the customer thoroughly inspects all business processes relative to the ownership of intellectual software including how information is obtained, roles of access, dissemination of private information, etc. The auditor may examine the contents of computer hard disks and the protection of intellectual property. If the customer has access control, the audit can be conducted offsite allowing representatives of the company to remotely check the computers of the outsourcer. Once a customer conducted an audit by remote access to the outsourcer's computers and, although the intellectual property was stored securely, it was discovered that one of the employees was working on projects for another employer during working hours. That employee was fired.

Intramural audit. A full audit is usually conducted every two years. Notice of an audit is usually given to an outsourcer two months in advance. The outsourcer is sent documents that consist of written questions about various aspects of its obligations such as the monitoring of physical security (access to premises) and the control of information security. The outsourcer must prepare a full response to these questions. This is followed by a representative of the customer who conducts the full audit. The auditor has considerable leeway in interviewing any employee of the outsourcing company, seeing his computer, asking questions of the project staff regarding the method of information sharing and transmittal (like email and access to the outsourcer's database), what is done with the accessed information (like whether it is stored on a remote server or on the employee's computer) and so on. Employees of the outsourcer must be prepared in advance to respond to these questions.

Information system outsourcing is tied to the client system and is compatible with it. So, the auditor actually performs a dual examination. On one hand the audit is a verification of the outsourcer's processes. But, on the other hand, it looks at the management of the transmission of information related to secondary work. For example, an outsourcer customer transmits certain required information. But, the required information is buried among other information in a larger document. Based on the "need-to-know" principle, the outsourcer should receive only selected parts of the document – those containing the required information. But the outsourcer customer's staff is lazy and sends the outsourcer the full version of the document, thus violating information security.

The auditor examines the outsourcer's practice of printing internal documents. What is the procedure for allowing electronic data to be copied to external drives and media such as flash drives? This is very difficult to check, but the auditor tries by asking the staff many questions. It should be noted that working on information material outside of the office is not necessarily prohibited. Sometimes the client allows employees to work on outsourcing from their homes. For example, if due to time zone differences it is more convenient to respond to a call from a client after working hours then the employee must have the materials on hand at home. The auditor in that case reviews rules related to the removal of information from the office. Readers who work in the field of conventional, open technologies may wonder what is so special about taking information home. And, those who work in the field of dual-use technologies may be surprised that it may be possible to take information out of the office. Usually, the customer simply specifies the rules that must be followed in cases such as these and the auditor verifies compliance with those rules.

Also, the auditor looks at how badges are stored and whether the badges of laid-off or terminated employees are destroyed. He checks the storage method for electronic devices, which are part of the access code for databases. And, the auditor reviews the system of access to the buildings where the offices of the outsourced work are located.

The auditor may refer to the list of pre-submitted questions and, perhaps, ask questions randomly. For example, he might ask "What is the procedure for entry into the office at night?" "What are the rules for the use of mobile phones with cameras?" "What is the procedure for access to the room where the server and firewall are located?" It is very good to have a set of written procedures that govern these issues. That makes a good impression on the auditor. However, if the auditor asks an employee at random about whether he is familiar with the document and the employee responds that he has no idea what the auditor is talking about, then that is a problem! In this regard, the auditor might be asked to verify that the appropriate documents have been communicated to the staff. Proof of this would possibly be copies of emails with an address list or an acknowledgment form with the signature of the employee, certifying that the employee has read the document.

It is common situation in Russia that people who are perceived to be important are often allowed entry into a facility without anyone asking who they are or demanding proper documents. This is an attribute of the Russian mentality. The staff security guard at the facility entrance should be instructed that auditor must follow standard procedures including registering as a visitor and presenting the proper documents.

Problems that are often revealed by an audit. Imagine that the auditor discovers that one of the names in the list of employees is written in English in three different ways and also appears that way in the document for an export license. The auditor wants to rectify this issue. The employee is called in and his passport is requested. It turns out that the last name in the U.S. visa is in the third spelling version. The auditor requires an explanation. All of this takes about forty minutes, and then you realize that you are very lucky with this auditor. After all, he has a plane ticket for the next day and does not want to linger a moment longer in your city. The conclusion was reached that the problem detected is simply one of misspelling. You fix it gallantly and he states that you are fully audited and that you have satisfied all of the rules of intellectual property protection.

However, let's talk about some of the not-so-obvious problems identified during the audit. Outsourcers often find themselves in this situation: the same computers on which they are working stores information for different customers. Therefore, it is not possible to provide the auditor with access to this computer because it is the obligation of the outsourcer to protect the information of the other customers from prying eyes. There are situations where an outsourcing employee works part of the day on one project and another part on another project or he may even work on it in another place. (Note that working simultaneously in two competing companies is prohibited, and it is discouraged even if the companies are non-competing.) It turns out that the same person has a right of access to the premises of two companies. As a general rule this is apparently not prohibited, but it does create additional complications with respect to customer audits.

It might be that at one time the employee needed a one-time access to certain information. This access was granted and then was to be closed, but someone forgot to do it. The auditor will note that this is a violation.

In addition to a direct examination, the auditor reviews in detail the organized work flow of the outsourcer and, in doing so, learns a great deal. However, the auditor may indicate that other identified issues or problems are not within the scope of its verification responsibilities. In one case auditors discovered wires lying on the floor in a manner that caused employees to stumble. In this case it would not be acceptable to argue that this was beyond the scope of responsibilities of the auditor and the problem must be corrected.

The auditor leaves the outsourcer with a list of deficiencies that must be corrected and allows it a reasonable period of time to make the corrections. Serious violations are given special attention.

In most cases it is unlikely that the auditor identifies anything so terrible as to cause the contract to be terminated. This is a situation that outsourcers who want to try to meet customer requirements want to avoid like the plague because in that case they would lose everything at one time. If the outsourcing firm provides a unique service to the customer, then the auditor should be prepared to recognize this and the possibility of the former losing the customer is lessened.

Finally, speaking about a full-time audit, we note that much depends on the individual auditor and they are all different. Here are some real stories about them. One auditor was a former policeman who, before working in the field of corporate information security, worked in various departments of the police department for 25 years. He loved telling stories from his past life as a policeman and all stories ended the same way: "And for that I had him arrested," causing horror among all of his listeners. Thus, this auditor is a product of his behavior that was developed over many years in the police department and that included not only matters in his core area of responsibility but also other areas such as fire safety, which in Russia has traditionally been ignored. Thanks to the auditor's intervention, an escape route was organized on the premises of the outsourcer, who had previously (according to Russian tradition) locked an exit with a key that was stored in a non-obvious place. In the event of a fire, this exit would have been blocked.

Of course, auditors are just people who have their own preferences and weaknesses. I must say that many outsourcers have been successful in actively entertaining the auditors and indulging their little weaknesses. The easiest way to "soften the heart" of an auditor, of course, is to feed him in a good restaurant. One classic example is that of an auditor who was invited to dine at one of Moscow's restaurants and said that he could dine for a half-hour only. But, he enjoyed the restaurant so much, that he called his assistant and cancelled the previously scheduled meetings. Then, he enjoyed a long and pleasant meal, having tried a good half of the available range of dishes.

Another auditor once had dinner with us in a prestigious restaurant. Naturally, the guest had to be entertained with conversation and, among other things; we noted that at one of the neighboring tables a well-known Russian TV personality was seated. It should be noted that the broadcaster behaved very modestly and was not singled out by the wait staff among other patrons. But, the more colorful members of another dinner party brought to mind the movie "The Godfather" because by contrast they enjoyed the increased attention of the waiters. After the dinner the restaurant owner brought a book of honorable guests of the restaurant to the table and asked the guests to sign it and then asked for permission to be photographed with the guests. Looking at this the auditor asked "If over there is seated a well-known Russian TV personality and no one pays him attention then who are these people?" We could not answer the question, of course, because this was the first time in my life that we had witnessed this type of "Cosa Nostra" behavior. We began to "interrogate" the waiters. The first four men politely declined to answer because it was confidential information. But, the fifth waiter "spilled the beans." It was the prince and princess of one of Europe's ruling houses!

But, it is not always easy to put the auditor in a good state of mind so that there will be a positive outcome. Sometimes the situation is more complex. In one case in our office in St. Petersburg we had an auditor who was very reserved emotionally. He did not seem to have any weaknesses. Good food? He was indifferent. Things to do? He did not seem to enjoy them. Praise? He only responded politely. Well, he was like the Terminator from the movie. But, once at the conference we saw the flash of a picture in his notebook. It was a Harley Davidson motorcycle. The next day the vehicle that the auditor was riding in "accidently" stopped in front of a shop that sold Harleys. I cannot honestly remember what excuse we used to stop there, but the auditor said that he wanted to go into the shop, where we spent two hours. When he left the shop he was in good spirits and told us that in Russia Harleys are much more expensive than in the U.S., but in general he was very pleased. In his report he wrote that everything was fine, we were fine and that the company was excellent as always.

The customer may require auditing the list of people who have access to the office. It often happens that a person is retired but continues to have access to the premises. Sometimes the access to premises is managed directly by the customer. Of course, it controls access only to those rooms where work is being done on its projects. The customer activates and cancels the badges for access to these rooms. It must be verified that the request to cancel the badges was sent on time and that access to persons who got quit is actually closed.

Self-test. Between full-time audits the outsourcer should conduct an annual self-test. The customer sends the outsourcer a document that describes a step-by-step procedure for self-auditing. As a rule, it says that all employees should read the plan for the control of the technology and other regulatory documents and should ensure that they are correctly implemented. As a result of this self-test, the outsourcer prepares a report and sends it to the customer.

CHAPTER 3

THE FINANCIAL MODELS OF OUTSOURCING

In this chapter we will consider the most common financial model of outsourcing that involves:

- Fixed cost
- Time and materials
- Transaction based
- Dedicated (offshore) development center

3.1 Fixed Cost Model

In organizing the outsourcing of business under this model, the customer assigns the outsourcer a specific project. The client is very knowledgeable about the nature and the scope of the work and can accurately describe what it wants as a result. An executive of the customer clearly negotiates the terms of performance and the workload with the outsourcer.

An advantage of this model is that price is determined in advance; the customer knows the parameters of the project. The outsourcer in this case assumes some risk if the project becomes more expensive. But, on the other hand, it will make a profit if the project is implemented quickly and inexpensively.

In one case a sales specialist in the IT field named John (name changed) was working at a small, recently started company trying to get it a good order for a project. Investors funded the customer company. It had a limited budget and tried to get the most for its money. Negotiations were long and hard. John spent a lot of effort but finally received the order. He went to his boss, the CEO of the outsourcing firm, and said "I've got good news, we have an order! But, it will not be easy. Our customer is not rich so it watches its money carefully. It was so difficult to work with them that we had to increase our costs of the project by 25%."

There is a subset of the fixed cost outsourcing model in which, depending on the timing or quality of the work performed, the outsourcer might receive a bonus.

Here is an example, suppose that the post office wants you to develop a software program that reads handwriting so that the processing of addresses on envelopes is speeded up. The customer and the developer stipulate in advance that the standard is a certain percentage of successful identification of text and puts in the contract that when a certain percentage of recognition is achieved the developer receives a bonus, but if it is not achieved it must pay a penalty. In this case, there is a clear criterion for determining the level of quality – the percentage of recognition of text. However, in many cases qualitative results cannot be defined as well so the "premium" approach does not apply.

In this model details of the project are determined prior to beginning work, however, there are times when price is subject to change during the term of the contract. Here is an example. Imagine the production of solar panels. Currently, only about 10% to 12% of solar energy is converted to electricity in these panels; the rest is dissipated as heat. Suppose that the customer is trying to develop a new model of solar panel that will achieve 15% efficiency, i.e. 15% of solar energy is converted to electricity. The developer enters in to a contract to develop the new technology for the panels and the contract provides a bonus or premium if the efficiency level reaches 16%. But, suppose that during the performance of the work it is learned that achieving an efficiency level of 16% is not realistic with the current state of technology. The developer did everything that it could and developed the product in good faith. So, the parties can modify the terms of the contract so that payment of the premium is based on other criteria. Changes in contract terms do not change the nature of fixed costs and are, in essence, a variation of this model.

3.2. Time and Materials Model

This is the most common financial model of outsourcing since it requires relatively little customer commitment and allows flexibility in organizing work and, in particular, to increase or decrease the number of people involved in the project. This model is used if the customer cannot clearly define in advance how many resources will be needed for the project. The project may be more complicated than anticipated or, perhaps, the customers of the customer want things speeded up or other changes made to the project parameters. In cases like this the contractor is paid on a time-spent basis for labor and also for project equipment and materials.

The cost of labor includes staff salaries, including any bonuses, payroll taxes, office rent, telecommunication, corporate charges plus the cost of the personnel and legal departments, and bank charges and fees.

Materials costs include any required project materials such as equipment and devices such as an additional server. We want to call attention to one thing. The customer may request the outsourcer to acquire special equipment for the project at customer's cost. The outsourcer buys the equipment and bills the customer. In doing so, the outsourcer may add a small predetermined fixed amount or percentage as a markup. The markup takes the form of a payment for the purchase of goods or the service of delivery or the cost of currency conversion. The amount of the markup (fixed or percentage) is the subject of the agreement between the customer and the party that performs the work that provides formulas for calculating markups. Here is an example. The outsourcer buys 10 servers, the seller requires pre-payment. The bill for the servers comes to $100,000, but the outsourcer adds a markup of $2,000 with the funds for the purchase to arrive in just a few weeks.

An advantage of this model is that the customer does not have to waste time and resources worrying about the implementation and cost of the project. The downside is that the customer must have an effective system of quality control to ensure project performance. It is both a headache and a cost for the customer to have such a system.

The control system is essentially similar to that which exists in any organization. It must consist of reporting procedures, performance evaluation and a system of reward and accountability. The system must be jointly developed so as to work effectively in the organizations of both the customer and the outsourcer.

On paper this works smoothly, but in real life unusual situations arise on a regular basis. Here is the real life story that occurred in one IT outsourcing company. After several years working with an outsourcer who was in another country, the customer wanted to change a previously signed contract with that organization and hired the law firm that originally drew the contract to assist in this effort. In the past, the law firm wrote similar contracts and used them as the basis for a standard contract for this kind of purpose. One of the points of this model agreement concerned the warranty given to the customer. In it the outsourcer was required to provide free troubleshooting for a certain period. Of course, the customer was pleased with these conditions, but the outsourcer did not agree to the terms. It seemed that in this case the outsourcer was not fully in charge of resource allocation and the timing of project implementation. Although it is true that the customer shared responsibility for the quality and timeliness of the project with the outsourcer, the customer could redeploy engineers from one project to another at its discretion. In addition, in this case there was no formal provision for the acceptance of projects because project development was a joint responsibility of the staff of the customers who all participated in defining the roles of engineers and project managers, each performing some part of the project.

So, how was the situation resolved? One of the possible ways to solve the problem was to develop new procedures for the acceptance of the various parts of the project and for submission of warranty claims. But, in this case, the customer would have to spend additional resources to determine who was responsible for every problem that arose. Such an investigations, itself, could become a large project. In this case the outsourcer has worked with a customer for several years, so another good solution is to omit the item from the warranty provision in the contract because the outsourcer has demonstrated that quality performance is not a problem and the customer has other effective ways to ensure quality in the outsourcing model.

When using the Time and Materials model the staff is paid for its time.

But, as a rule the customer does not specify what kind of salary the employees are to receive. Accordingly, the outsourcing company is interested in paying employees as little as possible, which tends to cause high turnover because the executive in charge is trying to recruit young, less experienced employees who are more inclined to change jobs. Younger professionals accept less money than more experienced workers, but they also require a longer training period before they can perform at a good quality level. The responsibility for ensuring that the staff is of the proper skill level is borne by the customer. In complex projects it may take up to a year before a new employee performs at a 100% level. Of course, the employer would like the employee to be fully productive almost immediately, but that is seldom feasible. In many cases, the newly hired, inexperienced employee cannot meet the standards for the job and is fired. His place is taken by another equally inexperienced employee in order to save on wages.

The client is not interested in this staff turnover and tries to minimize it. In order to solve the problem a multi-level skill system might be implemented where there is a range of 3-5 skill levels, each receiving a different rate of pay. It is possible to determine the appropriate skill level of an employee by using such criteria as length of time since graduation from school, amount of related experience and other clearly defined skill level assessments. It is recommended that the pay differential between the most and least experienced employees be based on a ratio of 2:1. In this case the outsourcer becomes interested in hiring people up to a certain skill level because as the skill levels rise so do the costs.

In a well balanced pay system the outsourcer gets the same profit when hiring an employee at any level and has no preference hiring more or less experienced personnel. The customer can request to hire a certain mixture of junior and senior experts. It can influence what is beneficial for an outsourcer to hire by varying pay numbers for each skill tier. That is, over a period of time an outsourcer can earn a large fee for an inexperienced staff and therefore it would be motivated to recruit young professionals. On the other hand, for some the greatest benefit would be gained by hiring more expensive employees. By applying this kind of pressure on a contractor, the client is able to make the project less costly without losing quality. Adjusting the numbers so that it is more profitable for the outsourcer to hire the right mixture of talents does this. It is helpful if the client knows the prevailing wage level in the outsourcer's locality. In most cases, this information is readily available from companies that sell labor market conditions in various regions. But, a good report is very expensive, costing as much as several thousand dollars. Nonetheless, such a report gives the customer a good understanding about what percentage fee he needs to pay an outsourcer for salaries. With this information, the client is able to optimize a scale of numbers that determine the fee for each staff experience level.

In one case, a lower level manager of a customer conducted interviews with applicants in order to hire those applicants who had the demonstrated knowledge and experience in the desired area. The general experience of the hiring managers seemed to be less important. But at the same time, the senior management of that company instructed him to reduce costs and to hire less expensive employees. The situation was handled effectively by selecting young candidates whose experience met the needs of the hiring managers but that intentionally restricted the flow of those candidates who would require higher pay. Both levels of management of the customer were satisfied with this solution.

The fee levels for an outsourcer's staff might not always be fixed. The customer might allow bonus payments, subject to circumstances related to the individual work performer. For example, if an employee works on a single project for several years, the outsourcer might get some sort of bonus in addition to the regular fee. The additional bonus might be used to motivate the employee, but it could also be spent for other purposes at outsourcer's discretion. The outsourcer is not directly accountable to the customer for how bonus money is spent.

Here is an example, an employee has worked on a project for three years and the outsourcer has started to get a bonus for him. But, the management takes part of this bonus money (that was originally put into a general fund designed to be distributed to the employees eligible for a bonus) and spends it on a salary increase for an experienced employee. We emphasize again that in general, the outsourcer does not report what employees are paid in salaries or bonuses to the client because this is strictly the outsourcer's prerogative.

Another form of incentive payment is the quarterly developer fee. For most Western companies, it is important to track how much money the company spends in a fiscal quarter rather than in a month. Therefore, the payment of the outsourcer fee can take place as follows: 30% of the total amount is paid in the first month, 30% in the second and 30% plus an additional 10% is paid in the third month with the last payment of 10% being contingent on the fulfillment of certain conditions. For example, the performer gets the money if the customer is completely satisfied with his work.

There is still another form of incentive to consider. Suppose that a client wants to encourage certain employees but the outsourcer has its own bonus system. The outsourcer is not required to disclose the exact details of this system to the client. But, if the customer believes that there is a risk that the outsourcer will not properly recognize certain employees, it can directly pay the employees a bonus over and beyond the total amount of the payment that was agreed. Of course, this bonus is less the required payroll taxes.

Typically, the total cash compensation to the employee (salary plus bonus) amounts to 45 to 55 percent of the amount earned by the outsourcer from the client. The rest goes to pay other operating expenses including the overhead, taxes and other costs that will be discussed in more detail below, leaving a certain amount for the outsourcer's profits. Briefly, the bonus fund and taxes account for 10% of the costs. About 20% of the cost is accounted for by infrastructure, equipment (computer servers), office maintenance (security, cleaning, utility bills, and bills for telephone and Internet communication), accounting, marketing, legal and for other professionals whose work is necessary but for which the outsourcer does not receive a fee from the customer. The remaining 20% is the company's profits. That is a rough estimate, but it is a very typical cost distribution for an outsourcing company.

3.3 Transaction Based Model

This model is based on payment for a single unit of work performed. It is not usually used for engineering design. Examples of this model are call centers, or warranty service centers in which payment is based on the number of calls received or on completed orders, and service for technical assistance on the road such as when a car breaks down and a customer calls the company providing this service. The company has an agreement with a local organization to provide on-site technical assistance in an area closest to the client. Thus, the client does not have to search for immediate technical assistance but rather only has to call one number. The contractor receives payment for the number of kilometers required to be traveled for the technical assistance.

Russia has traditionally specialized in the development, creation, and maintenance of new software, but not call centers or centers of warranty services, which are often placed in India due to the prevalence of English that is spoken there. Companies enhance the service to their clients by teaching operators to speak in an accent that is typical of an American region, like the Midwest. This is to disguise the fact that the customer service is not located in the United States. There are people who will not use the company's products if they think that it sent too many U.S. jobs overseas.

3.4 Dedicated Offshore Development Center

The term Dedicated Offshore Development Center is used in a broad sense to refer to an outsourced business model in which a certain group of employees, in a particular office, are performing the work of the customer and are under its direct control. In this chapter we will use the term in a narrow sense, in relation to the financial model of outsourcing.

In this model, the customer pays for the majority of actual expenses: salaries, bonuses, personnel, payroll taxes, cost of the office maintenance, infrastructure, etc. In addition, the customer pays a fixed amount for each employee per unit of time (month or quarter). This is a fixed amount for the maintenance of corporate functions and benefits of the outsourcer.

We share the narrow with the broad sense of the term because in a broad sense a Dedicated Offshore Development Center can be financed using the model of Time and Materials. In some cases, by means of proper financial modeling, the Dedicated Offshore Development Center can even use the Fixed Cost model that we will discuss below.

Customers think of the outsourcer as "their company," since they make all of the key financial decisions relating to taxes, office maintenance, infrastructure, etc. But, they are not the actual owners of the business. In fact, however, a dedicated development center provides a very high degree of integration with the customer's outsourcing management process. Actually, the next stage of transformation of a dedicated development center would be an official branch of the customer. There are issues of remuneration in the conduct this model, such as how to assign what salary to whom, including bonuses, and also the issues of hiring and firing. But, the outsourcer manages all corporate function including accounting and the organization of office work. The customer pays for actual costs incurred.

3.5 The Transition from One Financial Outsourcing Model to Another

There is a familiar scenario when a customer works with an outsourcing firm. The first project is often implemented by using the fixed cost model, since it is more effective for the customer to lessen the variables related to the performance of the outsourcer. But soon this model becomes obsolete because the customer tends to clearly prescribe terms of conduct and operation of the outsourcer. This is more difficult to do in high-tech areas. In those situations, the manufacturing of the product can be a separate project that can be outsourced. But, there are many things that cannot be known in advance, especially if the projects require certain experimentation. Here is an example: software is developed to control certain equipment. However, the equipment, itself, is also under development and this is done in parallel with the software development. Any changes that the design engineers might make in the hardware might also cause changes in the software, which would require other technical processing tasks to be done. Finally, the specifications might change because the customer has its own "customers" to whom it sells its products and the latter might also change their requirements.   When this occurs, the fixed cost model becomes obsolete and the parties begin to use the time and materials model described earlier. This transition from one model to another can occur over a period of several months after the commencement of the project.

When the outsourcing company has a long and stable record of operating within the time and materials model, the customer gains a better understanding about how to manage the outsourcing function. The parties mutually understand what is required of them and how this should be done. But, there may be a need to improve the financial aspect of the model such as reducing project costs or improving employee performance.

When this need arises, the customer may begin to pay bonuses to the outsourcer's employees. Then it begins to pay telecommunication expenses and other expenses. Eventually, the customer finds itself paying most or all of the costs of doing business and making all of the key decisions including setting wages for the employees. But, because the senior management of the customer has only limited authority over these functions, it decides to shift to a Dedicated Offshore Development Center model and this transition, also, can occur over a long period - even several years – after the commencement of a project.

The next step is that the customer decides that it does not want to pay a profit to the outsourcer and instead, it actually purchases the outsourcing company; thus transforming it into branch operation of the customer.

It sometimes happens that the customer does not want to make the outsourcer executives part of its own executive management. However, because the outsourcer has worked for the customer for a very long time, he has gained considerable knowledge and experience concerning the customer's products and the technology required to develop and product them. The customer realizes how effective and coherent the work has become and again begins the process of transforming the contractor, from the beginning to the conclusion of major projects, to the basis of a fixed cost model (but on a different level), thus closing the circle.

Although not the decisive factor, choosing the best financial model for a particular situation does contribute significantly to the success of an outsourced project. Both the customer and the outsourcer will know that they have chosen and optimized the correct financial model when they see that the project is moving along smoothly and successfully.

3.6 Hidden Costs of Outsourcing

The direct and explicit costs of outsourcing include the cost of labor, materials, equipment, training and travel. But, in addition, there are hidden costs. Any accountant can determine what the direct costs are. However, many customers will find that the hidden costs of outsourcing cause an unexpected "black hole" in their budgets. But, there is a less painful way to learn what the hidden costs might be – just read this chapter.

In a nutshell, the hidden costs of outsourcing are (1) those costs associated with the additional work or services that that would not have been necessary if the project had been performed by local employees of the customer, and (2) an unexpected increase in the normal costs associated with the specifics of managing remote project. Curiously, these hidden costs do not depend on which financial outsourcing model was chosen.

Managing projects from a distance is more difficult and complex than managing the same type of project in close proximity to the customer. This, in turn, can create a higher volume of work that requires hiring more managers. But, this can significantly add to project costs.

Obviously, recruitment is a necessary function for any company regardless whether or not it uses outsourcing. However, one disturbing pattern is that in the outsourcing company turnover is often higher than in the company of the customer. For example, if the customer is an American company and the outsourcer is a Russian organization, the U.S. office will usually have fewer employees than its Russian counterpart. This may be due to differences in the labor markets of Russia and the U.S. – in America work is harder to find. In general, staff turnover can be expected and the cost of hiring each new employee is an extra cost. This will occur even if the outsourcer conducts thorough pre-screening of employees and has all newcomers meet with the manager during business hours for orientation. Therefore, each newcomer must be trained and the more newcomers there are, the greater will be the cost of training.

Some of the hidden costs of outsourcing can be attributed to unforeseen costs in the customer's infrastructure. The customer may want all of a project's development and implementation costs integrated into its own organization's cost structure. This is necessary for business success. However, it requires the integration of certain expenses, such as additional costs for organizational security. For example, in order to ensure that a key employee is not a spy or working for a competitor (or something worse), it is necessary to do a thorough background check on that person. It must be learned whether that person has a criminal record, whether he really lives where he claims, etc. It is easier to obtain this information in the U.S. than in Russia. In the U.S. the law is clear about what information is in the public domain and what is not. Information available to the public about a person, for example, would include whether the person has any criminal convictions, whether he owns real estate, etc. In the U.S. it is quite legal to access databases that contain a variety of information about practically anyone. There are companies that specialize in gathering this type of information.

In the Russian Federation, until now there has not been a common database with information about financial loans. Nor is there an official single database with information about criminal records. If a person simply moved from one region to another within the Federation, no one in the new region would likely know anything about him. In the absence of an effective centralized power structure, gathering this kind of database has been very difficult. Therefore, obtaining this kind of information from other sources will be very expensive.

In order to include the hidden costs of infrastructure and accounting, it is necessary to transfer certain funds to the outsourcer. It is more complex to transfer the actual work. This is because in the U.S. accounting systems are highly automated; but the automated systems are set up to deal with specific operations unique to U.S. businesses. Imagine if a customer wants to pay an outsourcer to purchase multiple servers. Because of factors unique to the Russian organization, certain things should be done in advance of the purchase and the delivery of the goods to the outsourcer. In Russia there is no sales tax, but there is a Value Added Tax (VAT). The American accountant must make several unusual entries into his system to provide for pre-deliver payments, a Russian address, etc. All of this can be done, but the U.S. accountant is usually not trained to do this and must spend costly time trying to figure out how to perform the transactions.

Outsourcing can increase the expense of a software license. The right to use the software both at the customer's premises and also at the premises of the outsourcer can significantly increase the cost of the license. Sly Russian programmers often try to solve this problem by locating a server in the locale of the licensee and then accessing it remotely. However, software manufacturers are not that naïve and usually require that the user of the software must also be in the locale of the licensee.

An interesting example is the product licensing company Oracle that bases the cost of the licenses it grants to companies on the number of people who work at the premises of the purchaser. Imagine the kinds of products that companies make that are integrated with Oracle products. A license issue arises every time that one of these products is sold. Large U.S. companies have a master license from Oracle and the purchasers of its products are probably already licensed, thus in that case there is no problem. Now imagine that the same company hires an outsourcer for some project. In this case it would be necessary to pay Oracle for a new license for the outsourcer.

It is clear that in Russia it is a common practice for outsourcers to use unlicensed software. Even the most law-abiding customers often turn a "blind eye" to this. Most of the customers, especially Americans, try to comply with the spirit and letter of the law, but this is often in conflict with reality when they have a need to purchase a product that requires an expensive software license. We recommend that you closely follow the legislation associated with this subject.

A separate issue is the outsourcing customer's need to control access to its proprietary information. This requires a balance between protecting intellectual property and ensuring the normal and effective flow of work. In short, access to information must be controlled and there are tools to accomplish this. One of these tools is the firewall that restricts or allows access to a program. The term "firewall" is used to refer to any device or program that prevents unauthorized access to equipment or to a network.

The protection of intellectual property is a separate item in the hidden cost of outsourcing. First, the customer wants to protect its own intellectual property. But, secondly, if the project is related to dual-use technologies, the Government requirements for information security dictate that the customer implements and monitors an effective intellectual property protection system. In any case it is necessary for both the customer and outsourcer to train personnel, such as managers, in information security policy and procedures and to carry out appropriate inspections. An export license is also a separate item of cost. Often it is not possible to obtain it without cost because it may be necessary to consult an external attorney who specializes in export licensing. One of the export licensing requirements may be more strict control over the access that remote employees have to customer information. This can cause the need for implementation of remote control systems depending, perhaps, on the citizenship of each employee.

The organization that wants to outsource work to Russia should understand that things will cost significantly more there: computers, servers, vehicles, etc. This happens for obvious reasons. Candidly, all of the additional costs can be attributed to corruption. This does not mean that the outsourcing customer must pay a bribe to anyone. In fact, the U.S. law is very strict regarding bribery and corruption, so that is a very important issue for every American company that outsources work. Recently, there was a news report concerning a couple of very large American companies that were caught bribing officials in Russia. However, those companies did then proceed with the execution of their projects in a law abiding way that removed any possibility of bribery. The problem is that many of those Russian companies that provide outsourcing services operate in an environment that is potentially corrupt. For example, those companies that sell computers or repair office air conditioning equipment may be faced with extortion from either official or non-official parties. This leads to the fact that the prices of goods and services in Russia have built-in an additional cost variable that is required for the reality of business survival in today's Russia. We mention this to explain why the cost of similar goods and services is higher in Russia than in the West and is one of the hidden costs of outsourcing.

The last thing that should be mentioned in this chapter is the cost of customs; and, as you might know, that cost is not simply the cost of customs duty. Dealing with Russian customs is a separate, serious issue that causes whoever "collides" with Russian customs as much pain as dental surgery and makes them want to take leave and go to some Caribbean island. There are, fortunately, customs brokers in Russia who will obtain the proper clearance. But, this will be a longer and more expensive process than would be experienced in the United States. The process of customs registration may require many documents and specifications, both on the part of the outsourcer and the customer. This translates into the fact that the staff of both sender and recipient will be required to spend much time and effort preparing these documents. For example, after a standard IBM PC that was assembled in the United States was registered with Russian customs, the manufacturer provided documents and specifications for the keyboard. However, soon it became clear that the documentation was insufficient because the keyboard was made in Malaysia, and therefore requires a separate document because it was manufactured by a different company in a different country. Still later another document was required because the cord attached to the keyboard had a tag that said "Made in China."

In summary, export licenses, audits, inspections and training are hidden costs that confront the outsourcing client. Also, costs associated with the protection of intellectual property, infrastructure and software licenses are more expensive when a company remotely controls a project. One way to look at the total of these hidden costs is that they are usually the equivalent of having to add one staff person for every 50 employees in the client's company in the country in which it is located.

3.7 Documents "without which we can't survive" – Invoice and PO

The title of this paragraph is rephrasing of a song in a Russian movie "The ballad of sport"(1979) which was released just before the Moscow Summer Olympic Games.

Russian readers will be interested to know that in many cases American businesses can ignore formal documents, but in other cases there is a great deal of bureaucracy that requires a lot of paperwork. For example, a contract can be in either written or oral form. There was a case involving a multi-million dollar export business that for years operated without any formal contract or documents. The U.S. customs did not require a contract and, in this case, the government taxes were paid properly.

On the other hand, American readers will be interested to know that in Russia, a written contract with a corporate seal is required. For example, in order to make an international money transfer, the Russian company is required to provide the bank with a copy of the contract it has with a foreign partner. Similarly, a contract with a corporate seal is required for exports to Russia and for imports from Russia.

In America, the requirement for documentation of financial transactions is related to the need to verify that the tax return is correct. In the case of outsourcing, the principal financial document is an invoice (in the IT field in Russia the English term "invoice" is commonly used). An invoice is usually a short document that is periodically sent to a client stating the nature of the job that was done and the amount that is payable.

While there may be no written agreement (oral agreements are typical for small projects), the accounting of any fees charged and paid is absolutely required for tax purposes.

In most cases, the customer uses a document called a Purchase Order, PO for short. The PO indicates how much the buyer will be paid for the goods or services provided. This is in contrast to a written contract between the parties that describes in detail various aspects the terms and conditions of the agreed purchase such as delivery time, what happens in the case of "force majeure," etc. The PO is a short list of what is purchased and the total amount of payment required for the purchase. This document is usually valid for a certain period like one year or one quarter, which might be different from a calendar year or a calendar quarter. It should be emphasized that the PO signifies only the intention to spend money, but not the contractual obligation to do so. In some cases it is the practice for the customer to issue a PO in an amount greater than is needed at the time. There are several reasons why this may be done. For example, perhaps there is a plan to increase the amount of work to be done during the year. It might also be the case that it is not certain at the time of the issuance of the PO whether the scope of the project will be expanded or contracted or even partially or wholly terminated by the customer. In any of these cases the outsourcer submits an invoice for the actual work done up to the event that the PO is cancelled by the customer.

It may happen that the customer does not provide a PO before the beginning of work, or that it might provide one retroactively. The vendor may get nervous in this situation and start a project without written authorization? Outsourcers should keep in mind that if the management of the customer says "Start or continue your work" and does not explicitly stop the project then the customer incurs a contractual obligation to pay for work performed, even in the absence of a written PO.

What if a customer says "I am not satisfied with the quality of your work," does not pay for work performed and the contractor disagrees? Well, the contractor can file a lawsuit and go to court. But, it must be kept in mind that a lawsuit is meaningless if the disputed amount is small because the cost of legal fees is quite high. In a lawsuit for breach of contract it is common for the amount of the claim to significantly exceed actual damages because of the peculiarities of American law. However, in many U.S. states, including California, there is a small claims court to which a party can refer disputes over claims for less than a certain amount of money, such as less than five thousand dollars. In most small claims courts the parties to the dispute are not allowed to be represented by an attorney.

Most companies try to adjudicate or settle any dispute that exists between them. The most common reason for actual litigation is violation of intellectual property rights. It is rare that there is litigation over a dispute between an outsourcer and an American customer over unpaid invoices.

The invoice term for work performed or for the purchase of equipment by the contracting party is determined by the agreement between the parties (again, this agreement can be oral). If the Russian practice is the requirement of requiring an advanced payment then the typical U.S. payment term is 30 to 45 days after the invoice date. But, companies can agree on different terms and in practice some companies make payment more quickly or more slowly.

In Russia there is a practice to pay bills in a much shorter time. Sometimes, inexperienced outsourcers require payment from a US company within a few days, even if there is no agreement to do so. As a rule, however, this demand is useless because in the majority of corporations there is a bureaucratic process that is configured to process invoices within 30 to 45 days and it is very difficult to accelerate this.

What if a client is late making payment for worked performed; the specified time has passed and the client has not paid? Unfortunately, this happens more frequently than you might imagine, even when the clients are large, profitable U.S. companies. A frequent reason for delay is not a lack of money or an unwillingness to pay (disputed claims excluded), but rather internal bureaucratic processes. In Russia it is an accepted practice to charge penalties beginning with the first day of delay. But, in the United States it is not acceptable to levy fines. Sometimes Russian outsourcers have attempted to negotiate contracts with customers regarding charging additional fees in case of payment delay, but we are unaware of any successful cases doing so.

In Russia, prepayment is a practice in situations where the customer agrees to buy some equipment for the outsourcer and those terms are included in the PO. In Europe and in the U.S., such payments are usually made upon delivery of the equipment. Thus, the outsourcer pays for the purchase of the equipment up front and then submits an invoice to the customer upon delivery of the equipment. But, it might take several months between the initial payment for the equipment and the time that payment for it is received from the customer. In these cases the outsourcer must finance the deal. But, the invoice can then include a markup (a sum in excess of the cost of goods) to cover the cost of financing and any possible currency fluctuations. If you recall, in the earlier chapter on financial models of outsourcing we discussed the practice of issuing markups.

3.8. Taxation of Russian Outsourcing Companies

At the time of this book is written, some changes to the Russian tax law in general, and to high-tech enterprises in particular, were being made.

Because in Russia outsourcing mainly applies to information technology, these changes are very relevant to outsourcing companies. In this chapter we will discuss the tax system in the form that it existed at the time that we wrote this book.

When you read this chapter it is important to remember that in Russia there is no progressive scale of tax rates that are unified throughout the country.

Well, one last warning, the topic of taxes is no less upsetting than the issue of customs. Russians are accustomed to living in harsh conditions and act as experimental white mice that squeal when they are injected with a substance but continue doing what they were doing anyway. Foreigners and other outsiders have long ago stopped trying to penetrate the mysteries of the tax system of the largest country in the world, scratching their heads saying "How can you do business this way and still survive?" There is no one answer to this question.

In the Russian Federation there are two main systems of taxation, simplified here.

3.8.1 The Basic Tax System

The company that works under the main system pays four types of taxes: payroll tax, value added tax (VAT), property tax and income tax.

Payroll tax has two components. The first is personal income tax which is a tax on the income of an individual. This amounts to 13% and is withheld each month by the employer from the employee's pay. "Pay" includes salary, bonus, and all other payments from the employer to the employee.

The second component of the payroll tax is social premiums, which the employer pays monthly from its own funds. These premiums are allocated to various funds such as the pension fund (including insurance and reserve), social insurance, and mandatory medical insurance (a payment to both the territorial and federal funds of Mandatory Medical Insurance (MMI) and a contribution of social insurance for worker compensation in case of a work related injury or occupational disease. The component of insurance premiums concerning injury depends on the type of work done at the company. For IT companies it is 0.2% of the annual income of the employee.

According to the general rate of insurance contributions as of January, 2011, the total amount of all insurance contributions is 34.2% of the annual income of the employee allocated as follows:

- 0.2% worker compensation

- 26% for pension fund contributions
- 2.9% for social insurance fund contributions
- 3.1% for the Territorial MMI
- 2% for the Federal MMI

The maximum amount of annual income of an employee that as of 2011 is used as a basis for taxation is 463,000 rubles (in 2010 it was 415,000 rubles). If the income of an employee exceeds 463,000 rubles then the premiums are charged only against the 463,000.

Previously, the rate of insurance premiums was considerably lower (26%). Since the beginning of 2011, there has been a scheduled reduction in insurance premiums for enterprise-software developers who have accreditation at the Ministry of Communication. By 2020 the rate will be 14% (re: Article 58-1 of Federal Law N 212-FZ dated 24.07.2009, as amended on 11/25/2009, for the insurance premiums to the Pension Fund of the Russian Federation, the Social Insurance Fund of the Russian Federation, the Federal Health Insurance Fund and the territorial funds of mandatory medical insurance).

The value added tax (VAT) is 18% of the gross profit which is paid quarterly by the company. The gross profit is defined to mean the difference between the revenue and expenses of the company. For IT companies it takes into consideration only certain types of costs such as rental, equipment, consumables (stationery, ink cartridges, etc.), and employee travel expenses. Exactly which costs are included in the calculation is often ambiguous. Also under expenses is included all those services in which VAT has been included. There are many subtleties in the calculation of VAT. VAT is charged on advance payments received and then is counted when delivery is made.

We draw the reader's attention to the fact that in Russia VAT applies to both goods and services. In many other countries VAT applies only to goods.

Because of legal and VAT considerations, a Russian outsourcer has two choices: either it operates under the simplified tax system (more on this later) or the owner of the company must be a foreign organization. Also, VAT is not charged if three conditions are met with respect to enterprise development and adaptation of software and databases:

1.   The software developer is a Russian company that has been accredited by the Ministry of Communication,

2.   The manufactured product does not pass through customs, i.e. it is transmitted via the Internet,

3.   The manufactured product is not used within the Russian Federation.

Special attention is given to the issue of VAT and travel expenses. Many companies use a lot of outsourcers, who all together have many employees who accrue a lot of time charges. Some of the time charges are for direct work performance while other charges are for travel time and expenses. It is not a simple matter to properly account for all of these charges. The idea, however, is to allocate as much of the time charges as possible to travel expenses because VAT does not apply to travel expenses. But it does not go well if a company shows that half of its budget has been allocated to travel expenses. In Russia what can be considered travel expenses is strictly limited. They include properly documented expenses for transportation, lodging, meals, car rental and actual travel time.

Depending on the country in which the person is traveling, there is a prescribed daily allowance for travel expenses. For example, in the U.S. this is $70.00 each day while in Italy it is $65.00 and in Taiwan $67.00. It is not known how this schedule was developed or by whom. But if that standard is exceeded the company has a problem. So, if a company wants to pay the employee something in excess of the standard in the schedule, it must invent creative ways to make the extra charge. Directly entering $70.00 or $100.00 for each day in financial instruments is not allowed. If the trip is in Russia then the allowance is 700 rubles. But, even if the employee is sent abroad, it is believed that one day of travel time will be within the country and he will receive 700 rubles, even if in fact he left the country in the first hour of travel and returned in the last hour.

If the outsourcing company pays employees travel expenses then every time this occurs it must solve complex problems, like taking into consideration any fluctuations in exchange rates. For example, car rental must be paid in rubles at a certain rate of exchange on the day it was rented. Someone must learn and then perform the calculations for this.

For comparison purposes, here is how travel expenses are handled in the U.S. There are two types of payments:

1.   The employee receives a fixed amount for all deductible expenses for each day of travel. Actual travel costs are not paid. This is called a "per diem."

2.   The employee is reimbursed for the actual travel costs including transportation, lodging, meals, etc. The employee can pay for most of these costs by using a corporate credit card. This is very convenient because it is not necessary to collect receipts for every little item, yet a financial report on the business trip can easily be generated.

Now, let us return to the subject of taxation in the Russian Federation and consider the remaining taxes.

The property tax is 2% of the residual value of assets on the balance sheet of the enterprise, paid monthly in advance.

Net book value of the assets is calculated on the basis of the norms prescribed in legislation for each item. Thus, the life of your computer is defined as 2-3 years. Net book value of assets is calculated on the first day of each subsequent month and is reduced each month by a depreciation factor.

Property tax at the outsourcing company can be reduced if the owner of the property (e.g. expensive servers) is the customer's company. In that case the latter has to deal with the taxation issue. The amount of the property tax (2.2%) horrifies Western outsourcing customers. It is a very great amount.

Here is an example; a typical Intel Corporation plant is worth about two billion dollars. If that plant was located in Russia the property tax on it would be 40 million dollars per year.

Corporate income tax is 20% of company profits (revenue minus expenses excluding VAT) paid quarterly. The expenses include salaries with charges to the pension and health funds, rent, Internet and telephone, depreciation of fixed assets, and travel expenses. There is no progressive taxation scale.

3.8.2 Simplified Tax System

In the simplified tax system payroll taxes are paid in the same manner and form; but there is no VAT or property tax. The caveat is that the costs of equipment purchased during the year must all be deducted in the current year. So, if you bought a computer on December 31, it must be written off the same year. There is no income tax under the simplified system. In the past, the insurance premiums were significantly below 14% and so as not to cause people too much shock the kindly Russian government granted a transition period during which a number of enterprises will be entitled to preferential tax treatment of insurance premiums. But, in 2011 and 2012 the rate is 26%.

The amount of payment for a single tax can be determined in either of two ways. It can be either 15% of the difference between "income minus expenses" (with quarterly advance payments based on the book income and expenses) or 6% of the revenue of the company. What a way to pay taxes, the company decides the method!

There is a list of companies that do not have the right to move to a simplified tax system. The list is quite long but it includes banks, insurance companies, pension funds, investment funds, pawn shops, notaries and lawyers, gambling enterprises and foreign organizations.

Also, in order to qualify for transition to the simplified system the firm must have no more than 100 employees, its annual income must not be more than 60 million rubles and the value of its assets must not exceed 100 million rubles. Most outsourcing companies in Russia fall under these criteria.

If a business is unprofitable then under the basic system of taxation the income tax will be zero. But, under the simplified system there will be a minimum tax of at least one percent of the revenue. Experience shows that if a Russian company reports a loss on their tax returns there will almost certainly be an audit by the taxation authorities.

CHAPTER 4

HUMAN RESOURCE MANAGEMENT IN OUTSOURCING COMPANIES

4.1. Recruitment in the Outsourcing Company

Before we discuss the recruitment function in an outsourcing company, we turn our attention to one important feature of the outsourcing business as a whole. No project is eternal – not even the most durable and successful among them. You can work for many years with the same customer, but it is a black day for the outsourcer when, for insurmountable reasons, the customer no longer wants to continue the relationship. Of course, in order to pick up the projects from the outsourcer whose relationship is being terminated, the customer must hire another outsourcer that can provide a team that will meet the new demands and challenges. If there is an outsourcing organization that can bring together a team that will work on the customer's projects more effectively then the "old" outsourcer might lose that business. The fact that the current team has worked on the projects for several years and was effective does not necessarily stop that process. Keep in mind that American corporations are specially trained in ways to do this. Of course, there are potential risks and costs to such a transfer and the transfer process does not happen instantly. But, these issues are not insurmountable.

The only thing that protects you in this case is the customer's belief that the outsourcing contractor will be able to cope with any problems, including being able to find new qualified personnel. It is important to accurately frame this outsourcing issue because projects have a habit of changing over a period of time. When the project is changed then the approach to its implementation must be changed and new professionals will be needed on the team. The outsourcer must be able to find these professionals.

It is important that the outsourcer understand what performance criteria are important to the client (the cost of labor is not necessarily the most important parameter). For example, when the top management of a large Indian Satyam was arrested for violations in reporting financial numbers in 2009, clients of the company immediately began to develop plans for the transfer of projects to someone else or they reconsidered the possibility of picking up the projects themselves. In that moment it was not certain that Satyam would be able to continue to pay employees their regular salary. The employees could have just run and looked for work in other companies. However, the situation stabilized within the existing company.

We now turn to the subject of direct recruitment. Hiring of employees is the key to successful outsourcing. The outsourcer should be able to hire staff better than the customer can; and certainly better than other outsourcers and competitors.

Depending on the outsourcing model, hiring an employee is done on a "on demand" basis. In the time and materials model the customer allocates funds to hire a new employee for a project and notifies the outsourcer. On the other hand, in the fixed cost model the outsourcer decides what additional resources it needs for the project. If the customer initiated action to hire a new employee, the outsourcer's recruitment search is based on a position description prepared by the project manager of the customer. It is also possible that the management of the outsourcer approaches the customer with a proposal to hire a particular employee or to increase the number of employees on a project or, perhaps, to invite a specialist in a particular field to join the project team. Sometimes outsourcers use a unique technique. They justify the hiring of an additional specialist on a part-time basis and absorb the part-time pay, themselves. Their expectation is that over a period of time the customer will authorize and pay the full-time rate for many similar employees. Typically, this scheme has worked quite successfully.

4.1.1 Ways of Finding Employees

Employees are usually found in the following way: asking other employees and their friends to recommend a person, looking for or placing and publishing online ads, contacting university faculty in relevant fields, and using employment agencies. All of these methods can be used concurrently in order to find a suitable candidate as rapidly as possible.

Using employment agencies is the fastest, but most expensive, recruitment method. Most employment agencies charge a fee equivalent to 13% to 20% of the future base salary of the employee, not including any bonuses. Sometimes the employment agency may require the exclusive right to search for an employee for any job, but there is disagreement about whether the agency or the customer should decide which employee should be selected. Often this requirement is caused solely the greed of commercial agencies and it usually makes absolutely no sense for the outsourcer to agree to exclusivity. Also, the agency might require payment of a fee whether or not it is successful finding a suitable employee. So, if you are looking for an ordinary engineer, the concept of search exclusivity and the associated payment method should be rejected. For the most part, outsourcing companies can be firm about this matter and because many employment agencies are competing with each other, they are generally forced to concede on this issue. However, if you want to hire someone to be the president of a company then you will have to retain the services of an agency that specializes in this type of search. Because of the nature of their specialization, these agencies (known as "head hunters" or "search agencies") often control the market. They are expert in the methods, techniques and tools that achieve success recruiting a particularly valuable specialist. Because of this they can name their own terms regarding the matter of exclusivity and payment.

From the outsourcer's point of view, the hired staff is a product; the cost of the recruitment search should be allocated to the cost of production. If the cost of the recruitment search is not covered by the customer, the outsourcer may try to save its own staff resources and instead look to satisfying this requirement via the Internet which, although cheaper, is more labor intensive and can take much longer.

As recently as a year ago, websites specializing in this service were free. But now those sites charge a fee to the employer in Russia. Still, you can buy instant access for a limited period, such as one year, to broad databases that list many hundreds of prospective employees. At the time of this writing, the main supplier of listings of staff professionals was Monster.com.

In addition to finding listings of potentially suitable employees in the personnel databases of these sites, you can also advertise for a specific vacancy. However, because of market demand, qualified employees in the IT field (programmers or experts in the field of computer simulation, for example) who are looking for suitable professional positions are quickly "caught" by employment agencies and as a consequence rarely respond to Internet ads.

Posted information about job openings and resumes can be read in the social networks such as linkedin.com or on Russian sites. By the way, in Russia there are specific recruiting networks on the Internet. Many people post information about themselves but do not update it. Or, they provide an email address but never check their mail boxes. Apparently, many people simply do not believe that any real communication happens on the Internet. As a result, an employer might find a seemingly appropriate specialist but then is unsuccessful trying to contact that person by sending emails or making telephone calls. Sadly, this kind of situation is the rule rather than the exception. There is anecdotal (but nameless) information related to this type of communication in the Internet. For example, recruitment managers tried for two weeks to contact a particular job candidate to offer him a job. Finally, they received a one word response to their emails: "Later." In another case, there was a search for a specialist in a particular discipline of optics. In order to do this we used the Internet to locate scientists who have published work in this area. As a result of this search we identified ten possible candidates along with their email addresses and sent all of them an invitation to work. Only one person out of the ten responded and that person did not initially accept the invitation to work – he only wrote a response. We still do not know why no one else responded to the letter. It might be a matter of the Russian mentality. As a rule, a Russian would prefer not to respond to a letter in which he is not currently interested rather than bother to come up with a polite refusal. Interestingly, the one person who did respond later agreed to our terms and successfully began to work.

4.1.2 Resume

If an employer places job advertisements on the Internet, the prospective candidates, in turn, post a resume on all of those sites. There are rules for writing an effective resume; in appearance it must be presentable and in content it must contain significant, meaningful information. After all, the manager who is selecting employees on the day that it is read has already looked at dozens, if not hundreds, of resumes. The decision as to which candidate to call is often made after reading the first paragraph of the resume. Therefore, the challenge for the candidate is to write a resume so that after just a quick look, the manager will pick up the telephone, call the candidate and invite him for an interview. As a rule of thumb, the person who is invited for an interview is one of the three candidates whose qualifications best match the requirements for the vacancy. There are many articles about how to write a good resume, so we will not repeat that here. Rather, we will mention just those few aspects that in our experience are the most important elements of resumes.

Executive Summary. The first line should contain the person's first and last name. If the summary is in English it should be made clear to the English speaking reader which of an otherwise unintelligible name is the first and which is the last. If the name is written in "first to last" form, then a space is used to separate the first and the last name. However, if the last name precedes the first then a comma should be placed after the last name.

Contact information is also part of the Executive Summary. This should contain telephone number and email address and any other information such as street address, city, state or province or territory, postal code and country that will enable to the manager to contact you. This may seem to be obvious and should not be mentioned in this book. But, we have actually seen many cases when critical contact information was omitted and as a result the candidate could not be contacted.

It is desirable, but not required, to formulate a goal to which the candidate aspires. In the next paragraph resume, which is the most important of all, you should distill the experience, knowledge, abilities, capabilities and major accomplishments of the person for whom the resume applies. All of this should take up no more than a half of a page. You should use the utmost of your creativity to write this paragraph because your objective is that after the manager reads it he will want to immediately hire the candidate!

After this you can outline the education and work experience of the person (or visa versa). Especially for employees who have a track record, it is usually better to first write about their work experience and then about their education because work experience is a key part of any CV. Work experience should be listed in reverse chronological order, i.e. begin with the most recent and then list other experience in descending order. If there was a break in employment between companies then the candidate should be prepared to candidly explain what happened during that period. Do not be ashamed about anything in this section of the resume. Simply be candid and honest. You should be able to describe your experience appropriately in just a few pages.

It is not unusual that there are certain discrepancies or points that must be clarified in the resume. Perhaps, for example, a person's education is listed in a certain way but the dates seem to suggest that there was a gap in his education. The impression might have been that he graduated from the university on such and such a date, but that was not actually the case. You should be prepared to explain these discrepancies during a personal interview.

Resume Format.   The CV should be nicely formatted but without excessive ornateness. Do not lead with a table format because that is too impersonal, but in a summary that it is very important. If the resume is sent by email then attach a cover letter to it. But, do not insert the text of the cover letter in the body of an email message. Rather, include the cover letter as an MS Word attachment (or similar format) so that it conveys the impression that it is a personal letter. This is important because an employment manager receives many, many applications and resumes via email and you want yours to stand out from the others. In practice, many employment managers retain their favorite resumes on their computer hard drive where they can be easily retrieved, even if a candidate is not invited to an interview in the "first round."

We strongly recommend that you back up the file when you send a resume by email. If you lose it you will have to work many hours to recreate it and the recipient will be annoyed that he has received duplicates. This, in turn, causes the decision making manager to associate something negative with the resume of an otherwise qualified candidate. A few words about the archiving programs: in Russia, the backup utility rar is used instead of zip, which is standard in US. It is not clear why rar is used instead of zip. Zip is standard on any computer using Windows and you have no trouble opening zip files. But, if you send a rar file to an American manager he will probably not be able to open it and you will probably not be able to access the file.

Once candidates are selected they participate in a thorough interview. Because outsourcing companies in Russia work mostly for Western companies, it is common for them to use English terminology – with certain variations. The process of interviewing involves several steps and is time-consuming, but it is very necessary. The selection process is designed to eliminate a certain number of candidates. There may be ten "starters" but only two reach the finish line and are presented to the customer. The customer interviews the two finalists and selects one to be the winner. It is important that the management of the customer participate in the interview process and make the decision regarding which candidate should be hired. They do not need to participate in all phases of the selection process – just the final phase. This process makes it possible to more effectively select a new employee for the project team and for that person to enter the team on a "fast track" basis. As a result of the interview process, the management of the customer already knows what to expect from the new employee and can help steer him in the right direction.

Most interviews are conducted by telephone. The purpose of this screening interview is first to identify the most promising candidates and secondly to stimulate the candidate's interest in the company. Usually, the person who conducts the telephone interview follows a predetermined interview format. The interview typically lasts from 30-45 minutes. The call can be made either with or without advance notice to the candidate. Advance notification gives the candidate a chance to research the company and to prepare better for the interview. On the other hand, calling without notification is somewhat like a stress test and some allowance should be made for the candidate's lack of preparedness or if the candidate seems ill at ease.

Regardless whether the telephone call was planned or sudden, it is better for the interviewee to stand during the interview. This aids in concentration.

The quality of communications at a distance is important because the projects are international and almost all project communication is done by phone or Skype. Therefore, in the telephone interview it is important to learn how well the candidate communicates in this format.

The interviewer should take into account any cultural differences in perspective and thinking of candidates from the various countries. For example, when an American is asked to talk about himself he will use self-praise profusely. When he is asked about his knowledge and expertise in a certain field he will likely respond that he is a specialist and that no one else in the world has the expertise that he has. In contrast, Russians who are asked the same question will likely underestimate their achievements and say something like "Well, I know a little bit about it."

4.1.3 Sample Telephone Interview Script Outline

Welcome. The manager identifies himself and his company and explains the purpose of the call.

General questions. (More on this below.)

Assignments for the candidate. (More on this below, also. This is a very effective way to quickly determine the level of the candidate's training.)

Information about the nature of the job. The manager should briefly talk about the company and describe the job and the nature of the job duties. This usually evokes questions and comments by the candidate. Note that contrary to the standard interview format, you should provide this information toward the end of the interview. If it looks like the candidate will be a good prospect the "story line" should be presented energetically and with enthusiasm and the conversation should be ended on a strong note with the interviewer positively commenting on the talent and career prospects of the candidate. If the candidate does not seem to be enthused about the job or company, then this part of the interview can be shortened, thus saving time.

Questions from the candidate. It should be viewed as a negative if the candidate has no questions.

Completion of the conversation. The candidate should be informed about the possible next steps in the decision making process and he should be thanked for taking the time to speak with the interviewer.

4.1.4 General Questions for Telephone Interviews

"Are you looking for a job?" Surprisingly, not everyone answers in the affirmative and some respond positively only after a period of hesitation. The meaning of the candidate's answer to this question and the following discussion will help to determine whether the candidate is sufficiently motivated to find a new job. Also, as a result of this discussion it will become clear whether he is currently employed or not. There are times when a person simply wants to explore the job market but has no serious interest in changing jobs. If a person currently has a job you must learn why he wants to change to another. If he has no job, then why not? Here is one example of how this works. An applicant for a certain job had a good resume, great experience in the desired field and so on. However, the biography of the candidate contained one strange thing. He moved from Russia to the United States and lived there for several years, even becoming a U.S. citizen. The candidate worked for a large company where he had fifty subordinates. Then, for no apparent reason he retired and moved back to Russia. The question is how could it happen that a successful man who has lived in one country for many years suddenly decides to leave that country (and his home) and travel to another country which is less developed and where the living costs may be higher? In addition, why is he willing to take a job that pays less than his job in the other country? His answer that "I was bored there" was not convincing. A well-paid man, living in New York is bored there so he drops everything and moves to

Russia? We are not persuaded that the man was simply bored, so we must assume that this person had a special, undisclosed reason for moving. Note, there are definitely cases when a candidate had a desire to move back to Russia and in most of those cases everything worked out successfully.

Top reasons for looking for work. Find out why the person is looking for a new job. Some of the more common reasons include that the project has ended, salary, being tired of uninteresting work, and moving from one city to another.

You should also find out how long a person has been looking for work. The answer to this question immediately gives you an idea of the person's qualifications. For example, there is a shortage of programmers in Russia. So, if a programmer there is out of work for a long while perhaps it is because his qualifications are less than desirable, or perhaps he wants too much in relation to his qualifications and the job requirements.

By when do you want to find a new job? The responses to this question vary a great deal. Some people say "I already have two job offers and if by tomorrow I do not have one from your company I will take one of those." But, sometimes they make the opposite response like "I need a job, but I do not want to start for another six months." The answer to this question, as in the previous one, clarifies the candidate's general level of interest in the job and the specific circumstances of the candidate.

What are your current responsibilities? Of course, the manager is already familiar with the candidate's job summary, but now his task is to learn more about the candidate. Candidates typically begin to talk about the technical nature of the project at this point, but the manager should focus more on the job knowledge and skills of the candidate rather than on details of the project which might be proprietary to the candidate's employer. But, it is appropriate to talk about the size and scope of the project and the responsibilities of other employees in relation to the responsibilities of the candidate.

Describe what you believe would be the perfect job for you. This is a very important question but one that is very difficult for most candidates to answer. You can ask the candidate to tell you the criteria by which he would choose the "perfect" job and to indicate his job preferences among maybe ten different jobs. This reveals a great deal about the personality of the candidate. Realizing that the perfect job might not exist, the candidate will likely discuss such differences as long term growth, specific technical areas of work preference, compensation and team related issues. Rarely are wages cited as being the most important issue. There are situations when you believe that the candidate has multiple job offers. One of the tasks of the manager in that case is to persuade the preferred candidate to choose his company by emphasizing the kind of job attributes that are most attractive to the candidate.

Tasks in a telephone interview. A good way to determine the level of training of a candidate is to present him with a few problems during a telephone interview. In order to do this you should advise the candidate in advance that he will need paper and pencil during the interview and that he will be asked to solve several complex problems. These problems and the solution approach used by the candidate can then become the subject of discussion between the interview parties. If the candidate has not been successful solving the problems, the manager will be in a better position in the later phase of the interview to discuss terms and conditions for the candidate. If a candidate has solved all of the problems, this is a great success and management must make an urgent effort to hire that candidate "now!"

The most effective way to evaluate and compare candidates is to give them all the same problem. But, it is important to understand that "word of mouth" may make these problems known widely. But, when solving the problems and a need arises to ask the candidate questions, the manager will then be able to determine if the candidate is able to understand and remember the conditions of the problem, whether he has the ability to reason logically and to follow a step-by-step problem solving methodology, and whether he is capable of extraordinary thinking (for this you can suggest problems that have fundamentally similar conditions but that require quite different solutions). If the candidate is stubborn and is determined to solve the problems, you can give them to him as a form of homework.

Some candidates may refuse to do homework and may demand to learn the correct answer right away. Another might say that he did not remember the conditions of the problem anymore after spending 15 minutes on a solution, anyway. Rarely, but it does happen, the candidate will refuse to solve the problem immediately saying that he did not understand that it would be like that. Such a response usually leads to a negative outcome for the interview. If the candidate agrees to accept the problem as homework you should ask him to send you the solution via email. Of course, candidates can find solutions for the problem on the Internet, but there are pitfalls doing this. There could be a faulty solution on the Internet. Even if a correct answer is found on the Internet, its logic must be well understood and appropriately "fit the question," otherwise, as in school, it will not work. After a few days, you can ask the candidate questions and you can make sure that he is well-versed in both the problem and solution details. It is not too bad if the solution lacks much structure. We once received a very detailed solution to a problem, but there was a suspicion that the solution had been completely plagiarized. A few phrases at the beginning and end had been changed, but the middle portion of the text matched a certain website 100%. The candidate was asked a logical question – not whether or not he had copied the solution (in which case he would have said that he solved it himself), but instead, he was given a link to the website that contained the solution. Following that we received an email from the candidate stating that he did not want to work for us. Here is another case from a category that we can label "fun." Six months after we gave a candidate a problem he sent us the solution with a note that said "Better late than never!" Of course, by that time the job vacancy had been filled.

During the interview the manager proposed that the candidate participate in an assessment center simulation activity. The purpose of the activity was to learn how the candidate would behave in various job-related situations. In one of the situations the manager calls the candidate and gives him a job to perform. He also offers the candidate a technical solution that would enable him to perform the task. But after the manager hangs up he realizes that there is another solution to the problem, one that is simple, fast and effective. The question was, what should the employee do in that situation? Decide to perform the job his way or perform the job as instructed? A candidate might try to remain flexible and say, "I'll call the manager and tell him that I have a better solution to offer." But in that case the interviewer provides him with more background information: the manager continues to insist that his decision be followed. If the applicant proposes a solution then there are two possible ways to solve the problem and perform the job. So, which is the best way, the way that the applicant has proposed, or the manager's way? The correct answer is the manager's way because he might have additional information that the applicant lacks or he may have other reasons why it is necessary to do it his way and not otherwise.

The result of the interview. If the results of the telephone interview are positive, the next step could be either another telephone interview or a personal interview. It makes sense to ask the candidate for samples of his work from projects that he completed and also a list of references. In Russia, the candidate is expected to submit a letter of recommendation. But, it is also advisable to call his references and speak with them personally.

If an employee is referred by an employment agency, the first interview is usually all that is needed. The outsourcing company might give the agency a list of questions to ask the candidate and also qualification tests that the employee must take. But, this latter is fraught with risks because the tests could soon be made public and then they lose their value in evaluating a candidate's qualifications. The test, therefore, should be guarded as carefully as any other intellectual property.

In many cases the final interview is conducted by both the outsource manager and by the customer. There are several possible outcomes. One is to not extend a job offer to the candidate. In that case further recruitment would be required. The outsourcer must decide the extent that this alternative coincides with its opinion about the candidate. The outsourcer might also try to negotiate with the customer about the candidate to determine what really should be done about him. For example, if the candidate did not fully meet all of the job requirements should he be put in "standby mode" while the search for a better candidate continues? It is also possible that the candidate will be offered a job but not the one that he had hoped for; however it is possible that the candidate will refuse that offer. It is also possible that the candidate agrees that not everything went smoothly during the interview and that the job requirements might just be too high for the salary offered.

Before offering a candidate a job it is important that the information in the applicant's resume be checked for accuracy and that it coincides with the information that was learned in the interview. Any discrepancies should be noted, as well as any other information that might require further investigation. For example, it might be noted that for a period of time the candidate worked outside of his specialty or perhaps the candidate changed jobs frequently.

4.1.5 Refusal to Hire

It is important to inform an applicant that a decision has been made not to hire him in a way that maintains good relationships with the person. There are situations where the applicant is not hired for a particular job, but later a job for which he is ideally suited opens up. Appropriate wording for this might be: "At the moment we do not have a position that would exactly coincide with your talents."

4.1.6. Probation

In Russia, the typical probation period is three months. During this period the outsourcer carefully observes the employee's performance and behavior. If the outsourcer is uncomfortable with the employee then the employment can be terminated, even if the person is otherwise a good worker and is acceptable to the customer. Under Russian labor law, it is easier to dismiss an employee before the expiration of the probationary period. After that it is immeasurably more difficult.

4.2 Employee Motivation

Russian readers will be interested to learn how to design a compensation package for employees in the U.S. and American readers will be interested to learn the same as it applies to employees in Russia.

All companies are interested in retaining well-qualified employees for a long period of time. In this regard, every company designs its own system of motivation and rewards. The motivation for an employee to join a particular company and begin work there depends on various factors which are purely individual in nature, i.e. how convenient transportation to and from work might be or whether there are other members of his family employed by the same company. Thus, in one case an experienced candidate refused a job with a company because he was advised so by his mother!

4.2.1. Bonuses and Benefits

In the U.S., as in Russia, the salary for an employee consists of two parts – fixed and variable, similar to Russia's salary and bonus system. The fixed part is the base salary of an employee which is constant (benefits will be discussed later). The fixed portion, which consists of salary, can be increased on a scheduled basis, like once per year, or when there are changes in labor market conditions, without being tied in to a specific date. In the U.S. it is common for an employer to increase the wages of employees by from three to six percent annually. In Russia the amount of increase is larger due to market conditions. A Russian employee would be offended by a salary increase of three percent, which is quite logical since the annual rate of inflation in Russia is from seven to ten percent.

The variable part of salary is an amount that is paid to an employee in excess of his/her base salary as a reward for successful performance by the individual; his/her work unit or the company as a whole. In America it is common that in a year when individual, work unit or company performance has been very good then a large bonus is paid. On the other hand, if performance has been less than satisfactory then no bonus might be paid. In the latter case the employee might complain to his supervisor that he was counting on that extra money (the variable part) and is upset that he did not receive it.

The variable part of compensation is almost always tied to the success of the company and sometimes to length of service and is factored with the help of different algorithms. This facilitates the motivation of employees to continue to work for the benefit of the company for as long as possible.

In Russia stock options are not commonly used to motivate employees. One reason is that there are very few companies listed in the Russian stock market. On the other hand, this is a matter of interest to employees that has developed over the past several years and that is evolving. But, the current economic situation is Russia is only a few years old, although it does seem as though it has been an eternity. Russian private companies use only bonuses tied to periodic appraisals, depending on an employee's length of service with the company. In Russia both employees and employers view compensation in terms of monthly income, while Americans view compensation in annual terms. We believe that it is best to pay premiums (bonuses and awards) to employees on a quarterly basis and that the amount of premium must be tied to the performance appraisal. In this case certification is an important tool for promoting good work. Employees begin to forget what the reward system is if the frequency of appraisal and payment is as long as every six months or a year.

In Russia there is some bias against the system of bonuses and awards; people want only fixed salaries. New employees have a hard time understanding that there is a system of bonuses that they are actually paid. Perhaps this is due to a 90 year old system of "grey" salaries. In Russia, "black" salaries (as opposed to "white" salaries) are salaries that are paid in cash to avoid having to pay government taxes. Grey salaries are a combination of white and black salary payments. During the period of 90 years many public and private companies in Russia did not fulfill their promise to pay both the premium and regular salaries and the employees were helpless to do anything about it. They could not count on the judicial system for help. So, many of the people who are in the job market say that they prefer to receive only fixed salaries in the form of cash and they do not want any part of it to be variable income. A fairly good number of private companies would prefer to use that system, i.e. permanent or fixed salaries with no premiums. Our experience suggests that a combination of fixed and variable compensation is a better way to motivate employees to perform good work.

The use of an effective bonus incentive system is especially important for outsourcers because of their need to strengthen the feedback loop between the customer, who is located at a distance, and the work performer. The outsourcing customer might want to take part in determining the amount of premiums or other benefits paid by the outsourcer. This desire is natural because the customer wants to encourage those employees whose performance is "good" by its perspective to the maximum extent possible. However, this can cause a conflict situation if you are using a time and materials financing model. In that model, the customer wants to pay employees of the outsourcing company generously to encourage optimum work performance, but the outsourcer wants to pay them as little as possible in order to maximize its profits. Some employees try to take advantage of this situation. They tell the customer's manager that they are dissatisfied with their salary and, in turn, the customer's manager puts pressure on the outsourcer who then has to pay his employees more money. Alternatively, the outsourcer tells the customer that it is an independent company and that it will not discuss the salaries of its employees with anyone else. Western companies do not usually allow themselves to interfere in the internal issues of another company such as the determination of appropriate employee compensation. However, the attempt to intervene might be triggered by the outsourcer's employees who try to influence their employer by referring the matter directly to the customer. This behavior is more typical of the Russian mentality and less so for the Indians and Chinese.

The question of whether the customer should get involved in determining the salary and benefits package depends on the type of financial model that is selected. If a time and materials model has been chosen, then it is not desirable for the customer to get involved; because this also begins to affect processes of the outsourcer's organization for which the customer has no responsibility and which the customer cannot take over. In this situation the customer should be limited to conducting a periodic certification of employees with the assurance that the results of the certification will directly apply to the awarding of periodic wage increases. It should be explained that the results of the evaluation are important, but they are not the only criteria in determining the amount of compensation that should be given to any particular employee.

Sometimes, customers can pay an additional one-time or periodic bonus to key employees of the outsourcer, in addition to the agree fee per unit of time. Technically, it looks like this: the customer determines how much it wants to pay to whom and then may add this amount as a small percentage of outsourcing overhead. The outsourcer then increases the invoice to include this amount and pays the bonus net of government taxes.

When using the Dedicated Development Center model, the customer directly determines and pays the appropriate compensation for employees; the outsourcer receives an additional fixed fee per person per unit of time. In this case the responsibility lies with the customer and the outsourcer does not care how much money his team earns. In terms of financial modeling, this approach is inferior to the time and materials model because it shifts financial control and responsibility to the customer, who is operating at a distance, but leaves the responsibility to organize and motivate work performance on the shoulders of the outsourcer. The time and materials model is usually used to facilitate a transformation of the remote work force into being a branch of the customer.

The word "benefits" is embedded in the Russian language to commonly mean non-cash employee compensation. Sometimes the term "benefits" is used in a broader sense to include all types of cash payments (other than salary). Benefits can include, for example, compensation for the cost of food, subscription to a fitness room and to health insurance.

Let's talk about the nature of benefits. Benefits in Russia are different from those in the U.S. In the U.S., the term benefits is also intended to mean paid vacations and paid holidays. This is due to the differences in the laws of various countries. In Russia "leave" of that type is guaranteed to employees, but in the U.S. there is no such guarantee. The size of a private U.S. company often determines the number of holidays an employee might receive. In large U.S. corporations it is common for employees to receive two weeks of vacation per year plus an extra amount for executives depending on their seniority. A frequently used formula for determining the amount of paid vacation for which an employee is eligible is that one vacation day is added for each additional year of seniority up to a maximum of, say, no more than four weeks per year. While it is common for untaken vacation days to accrue to the benefit of the employee, it is not permissible for an employee to work for almost a life time accruing vacation and then take the last several years off from work. More likely, the company will ask the employee to take his vacation by a certain date or it might pay the employee for vacation time earned but not taken. Also, the company might allow an employee to be in arrears regarding his vacation (using more vacation credits than he had earned) with the expectation that as time goes on the employee must correct this imbalance.

There is an employee benefit called a "Sabbatical." This is a one-time additional leave with or without pay for an existing employee in recognition for long service with the company. The length of this leave can be very significant, perhaps six weeks or more. In the case of some university faculty it can be as much as a year or more.

In the U.S., companies are not required to compensate employees for the time that they take off for illness – this has been called the "fangs of capitalism." However, many U.S. companies have a policy of allowing a certain number of paid "sick days," although this is a strictly voluntary practice. In fact, Wikipedia reports that 39 percent of American workers are not covered by any paid sick day or sick leave policy. When a company does have a paid sick day policy, the amount of paid time off for an employee varies with the company, but averages about ten days per year. However, all U.S. states have a program in which employees are compensated for time lost from work due to occupational illness or injury which is provided by the state's worker compensation insurance program and is funded by a tax levied by the state on the company. Many companies also offer long-term disability insurance, usually at company expense, which provides compensation to employees whose non-occupational illness or injury requires an absence from work for a period of time exceeding any paid sick leave they might have. Sometimes companies allow employees who have not used their sick days during the year to use them as additional paid vacation days. In the United States there is no formal process for certifying that an employee is actually ill. The ill person simply follows a company procedure for "calling in" his illness to his supervisor or the human resources department. If the illness becomes extended then the company might ask the employee to bring in a note from his doctor confirming the reason for the absence. This is not likely to happen, but it is possible.

Other important employee benefits in the U.S. are health insurance and pension plans. Sometime there is also a benefit that is associated with the employee's compensation in the event of layoff. However, as a general rule this benefit is not disclosed at the time an employee is hired because it would be strange to tell a person, upon the signing of an employment contract, that in the event his employment is terminated he will be paid a certain sum of money in excess of any salary due to him. Called "severance pay," this compensation is usually calculated at the rate of one week of severance pay for each year of service. Not all companies offer severance pay and even at those that do offer it, the circumstances of eligibility vary considerably. It is very unlikely, for example, that an employee who was terminated for cause (malfeasance or nonfeasance) would receive severance pay. Also, the amount of severance pay varies with the level of the employee whose job is being terminated. Higher level employees and managers would, in most cases, receive a greater amount of severance pay than would rank-and-file employees.

Besides the money, severance pay for employees can also take the form of the continuance of health insurance for a fixed period of time (as a gesture of goodwill from the employer). By the way, under current law an employer does not have the right to cancel medical insurance for a terminated employee if the latter chooses to continue to pay the insurance premium.

All of the above benefits are traditional. Unusual benefits include, for example, a company car, food and lodging. In particular, companies like Facebook and Google feed their employees quite well. Free breakfast is available in the company dining room beginning at seven in the morning. Lunch and dinner is also served. The food, incidentally, is delicious! The food is free but it is considered a form of income and is subject to income tax, which is the responsibility of the employee. But, the employers usually increase the base compensation of the employee by an amount that offsets the additional income tax so that the food is essentially free.

Generally, the taxation of benefits in the U.S. is not easy to understand. For example, if as a bonus an employee receives tickets to a movie then the employee will have to pay tax on the value of the tickets even if he throws them in the waste basket and never uses them.

Also, at Facebook there is an employee referral program where employees are paid a bonus for each person that they refer to the company for recruitment purposes.

In Russia, the list of employee benefits traditionally paid is not as long as in the U.S. They consist of paid maternity leave (mandated by the government), meals for employees (not taxable), medical insurance, gym and tuition reimbursement. In some of the more progressive private companies there are other benefits, as well, such as life insurance.

The system of health insurance in Russia is not as comprehensive as in the U.S., but it does have its advantages and disadvantages. The employer usually pays the full cost of the health insurance, which is about one tenth of the cost of similar coverage in the United States. But, Russian health care insurance does not cover dental care or the cost of optometrists and it is designed for only a certain network of doctors in a particular city. Thus, if an employee was in another city or country at the time medical care was needed, he might be left without coverage. Theoretically, in Russia the public health care system is free, so employees have access to free medical care. This system applies only to Russian citizens.

Traditionally, Russian companies put on many expensive and elaborate events for various reasons and occasions at their own cost. This is a kind of benefit in Russia.

4.3 Dismissal of Employees

Sadly, sooner or later an employer will have to fire an employee. As already mentioned, Russian law protects the interests of employees and it is very difficult to dismiss someone who has been employed past the probationary period and who chooses not to submit a letter of resignation. One of the ways out of this situation is to terminate the employment contract between the employee and employer by mutual agreement. In this case it may or may not be necessary to comply with the traditional two-week notification period, but all other requirements are met.

If an employee writes a letter of resignation at his own volition, he must provide the company with two weeks' notice and he must continue to work for the employer during the two-week notification period. Many companies put up additional restrictions, as well. For example, an accountant might be allowed to resign only after he has completed a quarterly report. Technically, these requirements are illegal, but many employees agree with them anyway. When an employee voluntarily resigns, the company must strictly observe the two week notification period and it must monitor the employee very closely. Even if during that period the employee causes the company financial loss or holds any company money, the employer is obliged to release the employee at the end of two weeks and only then can it sue in court to recover any loss.

At the same time, the labor law of the Russian Federation establishes a list of reasons why an employer may fire an employee without a two-week notification period; this is referred to in the contract between the parties. Among these reasons are: the expiration of the labor agreement between the parties (if a specific term was set at the time of hiring), the transfer of the employee at his own request (or with his consent) to another employer or a transition to an elected position, the employee's refusal to continue to work in connection with a change in ownership of the organization or change in jurisdiction or a reorganization, the refusal of the employee to work in connection with changes in working conditions, the employees refusal to transfer to displace another employee in another place or a violation of Labor Codes or other Federal laws by the employer.

Reference is made to Article 81 of the Labor Code (adopted by the State

Duma December 21, 2001, approved by the Federation council December 26, 2001, as amended. Federal laws of 24.07 24.07.2002 N 97-FZ, of 25.07.2002 N 116-FZ, of 30.06.2003 N 86-FZ, of 27.04.2004 N 32-FZ, of 22.08.2004 N 122-FZ, of 29.12.2004 N 201-FZ, of 09.05.2005 N 45-FZ, of 30.06.2006 N 90-FZ, of 18.12.2006 N 232-FZ, from 30.12.2006 N 271-FZ, of 20.04.2007 N 54-FZ, of 21.07.2007 N 194-FZ, of 01.10.2007 N 224-FZ, of 18.10.2007 N 230-FZ, of 01.12.2007 N 309 -FZ, of 28.02.2008 N 13-FZ, of 22.07.2008 N 157-FZ, of 23.07.2008 N 160-FZ, of 25.12.2008 N 280-FZ, of 25.12.2008 N 281-FZ, from 30.12 .2008 N 309-FZ, of 30.12.2008 N 313-FZ, of 07.05.2009 N 80-FZ, of 17.07.2009 N 167-FZ, of 24.07.2009 N 206-FZ, of 24.07.2009 N 213 - FZ, of 10.11.2009 N 260-FZ, of 25.11.2009 N 267-FZ, as amended., as amended by Decision of the Constitutional Court from 15.03.2005 N 3-P, determination of the Constitutional Court from 11.07.2006 N 2 13 - Oh, from 03.11.2009 N 1369-O-P) that reads as follows:

The employment contract may be terminated by the employer in cases of:

1. The liquidation or termination of the individual business organization;

2. Reduction in the number of workers or staff of the business organization;

3. Failure of the employee to perform the work expected of his position due to lack of qualifications, confirmed by the results of certification;

4. Change in ownership of the organization (in relation to the head of the organization, his deputies and chief accountant);

5. The repeated failure, without reasonable excuse, of the employee to perform his job duties, or if disciplinary action has been taken against him;

6. A single gross violation by the employee of his job duties including:

• absence from work without good cause during the working day (shift), regardless of the duration, as well as in the case of absence from work without valid reason for more than four consecutive hours during the working day (shift);

• reporting for work (in the workplace or in the organization of the employer or the facility where the employer on behalf of an employee must perform the function of labor) under the influence of alcohol, drugs or other toxic substances;

• disclosure of secrets protected by law (public, commercial, official and otherwise), which became known to the employee in connection with the execution of his job duties, including disclosure of the personal data of another employee;

• commission of theft in the workplace (including petty theft) of another's property, embezzlement, intentional destruction or damage to the property as determined by a valid court sentence or order of the judge, or by an officer authorized to consider cases of administrative offenses;

• violations of health and safety laws established for the protection of labor or the violations of worker safety requirements, if the violation resulted in serious consequences (industrial accident or illness), or knowingly creating a real threat of such consequences;

• direct commission of acts adversely affecting the financial and commodity values of the employer, if these actions give rise to loss of confidence in him by the employer;

• commission by an employee who performs educational functions of an immoral act that is incompatible with the continuation of this work;

• making unreasonable decisions by the head of the organization (its branches or offices), his deputies and chief accountant, which entailed a violation of the preservation of property, unauthorized use or other damage to property of the organization;

• commission of a single gross violation by the head of the organization (its branches or offices), his deputies, of their job duties;

• submission of false documents to the employer by employee with respect to an employment contract;

• violations committed under an employment contract with the head of the organization, members of the collegial executive body of the organization;

• other violations as may be established by this Code and other state and federal laws.

In practice, the dismissal of an outsourcing employee is not for any of the above reasons. The main problem in the dismissal of an outsourcing employee is that the customer may, without notice, declare that so and so person is no longer needed and that he should stop working on its projects. Here is the problem, should the employee be transferred to another department or should he be dismissed? Russian law does not allow a company to fire an employee just like that! It would be necessary to explain to the employee that it would be better for him to resign or, if that fails, then another cause should be found to fire him. In this case you can use the following dismissal method: the employee is reminded that the work day begins at 9:00 AM and that he must be at work on time. Being late twice or more is considered a violation of labor protocol and is a cause for dismissal. In essence, such a threat is a form of blackmail but it should be enough to convince the employee to voluntarily resign. In practice, this type of compulsory retirement does not actually reach that point. The employee prefers to write a letter of resignation that the employer can dismiss him at will and he will look for another job rather than "butt heads" with the employer.

Here is a real life situation. An employee, let's call him Bob, made a direct offer to a client to complete a project on which he has been working for a long time, thus bypassing the outsourcer employer. Bob probably thought that it would be more important to the customer to complete the project more cheaply. He considers himself to be indispensable to the project and thus calculates that he can dictate the terms and conditions of this situation with the client, although Bob was aware that the customer has successfully worked with this outsourcer long before Bob took the job. In fact, Bob has never been able to complete the project alone – he always needed help from his colleagues but he was not aware that this had been documented.

In short, Bob submitted a proposal to the client suggesting that the client could "dump" his employer, the current outsourcer, and that Bob could run the project independently for far less money than the customer was then paying the outsourcer. However, the proposal also indicated that there was a need to recruit other workers for the project and that Bob could arrange this. The customer's manager was very surprised by the letter but his reaction was predictable. He immediately forwarded the letter to the director of the outsourcing company with a request that he not dismiss Bob immediately but only after the project had been completed.

Upon learning about the correspondence, the director quite naturally decided to dismiss Bob immediately. The question was how? The situation was complicated by the fact that Bob was a man of confrontation and could easily go to court, which the employer deemed to be undesirable. However, Bob worked on the project on a part-time basis and in such cases an employer is legally allowed to fire the person with only three days written notice if the position is converted to the full-time status, but the employee declines to work full time. So, knowing that Bob would refuse, the Director offered him a full-time position. As expected, Bob refused and the director told him, "then I will have to fire you." Bob was enraged. "How can that be? I am the most important person on the project. I will write a letter of resignation!" The director told him to write… and Bob grabbed a pen and paper and wrote. He signed his resignation which was immediately accepted. Bob was then replaced by another employee and the project was successfully completed.

Another real-life example concerns the prerogatives of a state under American labor law. The state of California, for example, permits an employer to fire an employee without reason. Sometimes managers of companies in California that use outsourcers do not hesitate to disqualify and terminate outsourcing personnel at the "drop of a hat." Once on a Friday evening the director of a Russian outsourcing company received a letter from a California customer telling him that on Monday a certain employee of the outsourcer will no longer work for it. The director began to understand what was going on. It turns out that a manager of the American customer called the employee and asked him to immediately correct an error in the source code. The Russian employee refused saying that he had already left the office for the day and that he did not intend to return there because in local time it was the dead of night. According to Russian labor law, work in excess of ordinary hours can only be done with the consent of the employee. In this case, the American manager had reacted to what he perceived to be an unwillingness to somehow resolve the problem. If the Russian employee had calmly explained why he could not immediately return to the office and instead offered to go to work, for example, on Saturday then probably nothing bad would have happened and the problem would have been corrected. The employee in that case would have received compensation to work on the weekend. But, what happened, happened.

The management of the Russian outsourcing company was confronted with a difficult situation. They had an employee who would have to stop working on Monday because that was the day on which the American customer would stop paying for his work. But, according to Russian law, the employee was simply exercising his rights. What should be done? The director of the outsourcing company used diplomacy and convinced the employee to write a letter of resignation.

A lesson that can be learned from this example is that a well-trained staff should work with the customer collaboratively. Sometimes a negative conclusion to a problem issue is not due to something actually having gone wrong but rather to the fact that something wrong was said. An employee who wants to be successful must take into account not only his interests but also the interests of his immediate supervisor and of the customer. If the customer removes an employee from a project, the employer often has no other option except to dismiss the employee, following the labor laws of their country.

Here is another example. An employee was hired by an outsourcing company but did not appear for work on the first day due to an illness and was immediately granted sick leave. For the benefit of American readers, in Russia sick leave documents also contain a diagnosis. According to a list that is prescribed by the state program, the documents serve as the basis for the number of days of compensation that is paid to the employee. In the above case the diagnosis was very serious, although at the time of the interview the employee seemed to be quite healthy. The director suspected that something was wrong and tried to figure out what actually happened. It turned out that the medical certificate was signed by the employee's mother, who happened to be a physician.

In Russia, the doctor can sign a medical certificate that is valid for a certain period of time. The maximum duration of sick leave is governed by the state. If the treatment requires more time, then the physician has no power to prolong the amount of sick leave, but it can be extended by a medical committee. During the sick leave period the employer has no right to dismiss the employee.

In the above case, the disease was a "sham." The sick leave could not be extended indefinitely because the medical committee will require that it be concluded after a certain period. Consequently, the employee was forced to interrupt the sick leave in order to comply with the committee's directive. There must be a break of at least one work day between sick leave periods to restart the clock. On one of those days the employee was fired because his probationary period had not expired and labor law allows dismissal before the expiration of the probationary period.

4.4 Personnel Management in Times of Ups and Downs

Economic ups and downs are cyclical. Studies show that in America, since the Great Depression that lasted from August, 1929 to March, 1933, economic downturns do not last more than eighteen months. Speaking about the specifics of outsourcing, it should be noted that the outsourcing industry, itself, and individual outsourcing businesses might have their own cycle of ups and downs. For example, following Moore's Law the semiconductor industry replaces components every eighteen months. For those who are not familiar with Moore's Law, Gordon Moore, one of the founders of Intel, formulated this rule in 1965. According to Moore's Law, semiconductor companies replace equipment in their plants every eighteen months causing an increase in demand for the products of those manufacturers of the equipment. Then, after the replacement, industry demand falls off sharply until the next cycle.

In this chapter we will consider the problems that arise among the companies of customers and outsourcers in periods of ups and downs and how to solve those problems.

4.4.1 "The savings on coffee," and Other Ways to Survive Outsourcing during a Recession

Consider two contrasting examples: the customer is a small start-up company versus a large well established company.

Start-ups are not necessarily susceptible to fluctuations of the economy. They are funded by investors and keep working till the original investment is exhausted. When the money runs out or when the next portion of startup funding is not received the project can die. Thus, small companies can withstand economic downturns but, on the other hand, they can suddenly die overnight.

Large companies are subject to business cycles. In addition, large companies have different units in which cycles can be expressed in different ways. Sometimes the project teams that are involved in development receive funding and, in fact, an internal start-up may not be susceptible to fluctuations. However, it is possible that other units in the same company do feel the effects of an economic downturn.

Imagine that a recession is beginning in an industry where the customer operates. The company tries to predict the depth and duration of the recession, but it usually turns out badly. Typically, a company's business plan can forecast quite accurately for the forthcoming quarter. Bur it is often less accurate trying to forecast for a longer period. At the beginning of a recession a company may cut production and staff, but it does not know the extent to which this should be done. During the recession the company must be prepared to respond rapidly to business conditions so as not to lose business to the competition. The first thing that companies try to do in a recession is to cut costs. We call this period the "economies of coffee." The name is not accidental. In America traditionally the free coffee provided to employees is watered down and in periods of recession the coffee cream is replaced with vegetable powder substitute. This measure has more of a psychological purpose: to remind employees that the situation is serious and that there must be "belt tightening."

Are the savings on the coffee a threat to the outsourcer? First, the number of business trips to the customer site is minimized. Secondly, staffing requirements are reviewed; hiring new employees is stopped and vacancies are not filled, which is a rather painless way to reduced previously planned expenditures. The move to "save on coffee" may include the reduction of corporate sponsored events – for the outsourcer it translates to the elimination of customer paid English language lessons. If the above measures are insufficient and the economic situation continues to deteriorate, they begin to reduce the purchase of equipment, computers and software licenses.

American companies engage in the practice of "involuntarily vacation," also called shutdowns, forcing employees to take paid or not paid vacations. For example, every month there may be a practice of a one-week shutdown or perhaps every Friday operations close. Of course, during these periods of shutdowns the employees are not paid. If the employee has accrued days off during this period he may take it and get paid. The American accounting system is designed so that even if an employee goes on paid leave, the company can record a savings. But, in Russia, due to the nature of the accounting system this "vacation" time would not result in a savings.

The labor laws of the Russian Federation specify that an employer can send an employee on a vacation without his consent only if the leave was scheduled in advance. Therefore, in Russia this is not a tool that can be used to reduce costs.

In a recession, instead of laying off employees the contracting authority might reduce salaries. It is often advantageous to the outsourcer to accept a pay cut rather than to be laid off, which is also not an option in Russia due to the Russian Labor Law limitation.

What helps the outsourcer overcome a recession? Surprisingly, in the event of an economic slowdown in developed countries, the exchange rate will work in favor of outsourcing service providers. This is due to the fact that global investors view the dollar as the safest financial instrument. Therefore, during recessions the dollar rises against other currencies since savings are converted to dollars. The same is true of the euro, but to a lesser extent. Typically, the outsourcer is paid in dollars but pays its employees in the local currency. The increase in the value of the dollar compared with the local currency helps to increase the profits of the outsourcer during a recession and offsets the decline in revenue.

Another way to overcome a recession is for outsourcers to strengthen their teams. On the one hand, the outsource takes measures to retain key employees and may actually increase their salaries. On the other hand, it may reduce efforts to attract new employees. During this period more talent is available in the labor market and an outsourcer has a good chance to hire them. Where are the jobs? First, in an economic downturn there is reduced staff turnover – it remains near zero. But, someone always resigns and then the employer looks for a replacement. Secondly, an outsourcer can always hire a good professional at its own expense and then when possible put him on a team that is paid by the customer. As a result, by strengthening the team and showing the customer that the quality and productivity of projects has increased, the outsourcer can look forward to new projects from the customer and successful business growth. Further, the client continues to reduce their employment but the employment in outsourcing increases even in a recession. This is not a hypothetical situation. Experience shows how well this approach works.

And finally, we must believe that after every recession there will be a recovery.

4.4.2 Problems Confronting Outsourcers in Economic Boom

Decline is followed by a rise and then the outsourcer is faced with a different set of problems; the most serious is staff turnover. Employers tend to recruit each other's talents so in time staff turnover might reach 20 percent or more. The customer, in turn pressures the outsourcer to reduce turnover. In such a situation the outsourcer often introduces additional benefits (for example, it might pay a gym membership for employees) and it periodically increases the salaries of key personnel, or even of the entire staff, and uses foreign travel as a form of incentive. When all methods are exhausted, the outsourcer may appeal to the customer with a request to raised work rates. Typically, customers are forced to accept an increase in rates. Sometimes it works this way: the customer pays a fee for every employee who has worked for the outsourcing company for certain number of years. The outsourcer uses these funds to increase wages in the hope of retaining long service employees.

On one hand, a twenty percent turnover rate, which is typical among outsourcers in India and Russia, allows the outsourcer to work steadily. For Western managers, such turnover is too high, however. Now, apply a mathematical calculation to this situation. Suppose that the number of employees leaving over a period of time is subject to a Poisson distribution. One of the most famous examples of a Poisson distribution (a discrete probability distribution to model the number of events that will occur over a given period of time) was the number of soldiers in the Prussian cavalry killed by an accidental blow of the horse's hooves in one year.

Assuming a Poisson distribution, a twenty percent turnover rate means that employees on the average work at the same place for five years. One would agree that this average expectancy looks quite good. If turnover remains within this magnitude it is not a problem. But if the percentage exceeds this value, then the cause of the problem must be identified and corrected. Typical reasons for employees leaving their employment are that the work is not interesting; there is a lack of opportunity for advancement, low pay, etc. Employees often think that if they go to their boss and threaten to leave unless they receive a pay increase that it will work. Suppose that over time the skills of an employee are increasing and that he deserves a raise. However, outsourcing personnel should perform a project for a certain amount of money. When this is done there is a good balance between expensive and less expensive workers. This balance is dictated by the nature of the project. The employer is interested on the one hand to retain key employees and on the other hand to maintain this balance. In this case, the turnover rate is used as a tool that supports this balance at a certain level.

Strictly speaking, during an economic downturn the problem of staff turnover also exists, though it is not as prevalent. The fact is that projects are often managed by managers of the customer and employees of the outsourcing company. This does not leave many career growth opportunities for the outsourcing contractor. He can become a team leader or a project leader, but it ends there. This situation fosters turnover because at some point people want to experience career growth and they will start to look for those opportunities outside of the particular company. In some respects, this problem is solved by the customer; in order to create new groups and projects there will be new jobs for project leaders.

As we mentioned above, the rate of a national currency against the dollar and the euro is rising. Investors are investing in risky assets by selling dollars. In boom periods the dollar does not favor the outsourcer. Large Western corporations can buy certain financial instruments to be a "hedge" against the dollar. This is an internal way to compensate for exchange rate fluctuations.

4.5. Methods for Performance Evaluations

Let us say that a well-defined, formal way to evaluate the work of an employee outsourcing company does not exist.

The purpose of evaluating the staff is to create a performance review system that will link the degree of customer satisfaction with the motivation and performance of the employees. As with any business, if the customer is satisfied, then the business is successful. On one hand it is necessary to keep abreast of feedback from the customer. On the other hand, it is necessary to motivate employees to respond to what the customer says. How can this be applied to outsourcing? The answer is simple. You have to periodically survey the managers of the customer to determine whether they are satisfied with the work of each member of the outsourcer's team. In essence, you have to train long and hard to understand the needs of the customer and to respond to those needs. If the customer's employees are not accustomed to, or do not want to, engage in this process then we must repeatedly explain that the quality of the project depends on effective customer feedback. Further, we must explain that working with the remote outsourcing staff requires a more thorough and frequent assessment that would be necessary for local teams. The assessment process is very simple and should take no longer than just a few minutes per person. If this is adhered to then the customer will not say that the certification process is done too frequently or that it is a time consuming process. Sooner or later the managers of the customer will become accustomed to this periodic assessment and the system will become self-sustaining.

Periodic assessment is required of the increased responsibilities of both parties, both customer and outsourcer. The contractor will know that his work is appreciated and that it will be recognized, perhaps via a bonus. The customer, in turn, knows that it must ensure that the work of the contractor is done and then it must assess the work, otherwise the contractor will lose the bonus. The frequency of the performance reviews should coincide with the periodic payment of bonuses. It is recommended that the review be conducted on a frequency of not less than once every three months. Once per year is too infrequent and will cause a loss of the important interpersonal dynamics that are essential for both management and staff to effectively assess work performance.

Sometimes the outsourcer instructs its project leaders to conduct similar performance reviews for their subordinates and then take into consideration the cumulative assessment by both themselves and the customer. This increases the role of project leaders, allowing them to influence the bonuses for their employees.

We recommend the following options for the certification of personnel:

1. On time Delivery – the timeliness with which each employee delivers the job that is assigned to him,

2. Satisfying Requirements – how well the employee performs the required work. Here is a real-life example. The outsourcer had to produce a semiconductor circuit. Among other things he was asked to produce an output voltage of 5 volts. The customer received a sample to be tested and learned that the output voltage was 4.9 volts. The contractor said: "But, this is almost the same thing." The customer did not accept that explanation and the assignment had to be redone. Strictly speaking, the customer could have allowed a tolerance in the specifications. But, we know that the customer is always right.

3. Quality – this is a subjective parameter that is not always possible to formally describe. Well-made software is one that works without errors and for which there is good documentation. Unfortunately, in complex systems the quality of work is revealed only after a long period of time and interim tests do not detect all of the possible problems. It is often very difficult to determine what kind of mistake is made by a particular performer. Nonetheless, it is advisable to use this option, even considering all of its subjectivity.

4. Quality of Documentation - this includes the quality of communication between the contractor and the manager. In outsourcing communication takes place at a distance. It is important that the staff have the time to report their problems and needs and the time to report on work performance, etc. It might sound like a trivial issue. But, communication difficulties happen so often that this must be mentioned. Further, poor communication is the most frequently mentioned reason why a customer wants to fire a contractor and replace him with someone else.

5. Innovation – the extent that the employee takes the initiative and how useful his initiative is. This also is a very informal and subjective metric, however it motivates the employees to come up with new, innovative solutions.

Each of these criteria should be given a score on a scale from 1 = very bad, 2 = below average, 3 = average, 4 = very good, 5 = exceptional quality of work. Individual assessments should be communicates to the employee. It is advisable to use the average score to determine a level for the employee and the average to calculate a group score to determine the group leader bonus.

Let's talk about the subjectivity of any assessment system. On the one hand, the customer makes a subjective assessment. On the other hand, the outsourcer subjectively considers these assessments to help him determine a bonus for each employee. There is no mathematical formula that would allow someone to deduce a specific percentage bonus for each employee. Curiously, employees often believe that the employer does use an exact formula and they are surprised when the amount of their bonus deviates from what they had expected, despite the fact that their management had periodically stressed that the amount of the bonus depends on a number of both objective and subjective reasons.

The customer can give all team members the same rating for a limited time and that rating might be correct. However, over the long term it is inevitable that situations will arise when the customer will want to differentiate among employees and a well-established system would be an excellent tool for this. We call the reader's attention to one rating aspect; as a rule, customers tend to perceive the employee with whom it has the most direct contact in a teleconference as being the best performer and then rates that employee accordingly. The issue becomes more complex when the nature of the outsourcing involves other people in addition to the main contractor or work performer. In this case it can be a problem for the management of the outsourcer to ensure that all of the project teams are properly motivated.

When the customer's project manager is changed it could result in a small difference in the absolute level of ratings; the new manager has his own subjective opinion of the work. This difference should not cause a major change in the motivation of the outsourcing company's employees.

As can be seen by these examples of the subjective nature of assessments for bonus purposes, some type of "leveling" system is needed to smooth out the rating variances. The assessment criteria described above, used by the management of both the customer and the outsourcer, can serve as that tool.

The system allows for the collection of assessments that can be used to analyze the trend of each measurement parameter or to assess the dynamics of customer satisfaction in general. We emphasize that based on many years of experience we have reached the conclusion that periodic certification is an effective business development tool. Based on the assessments, the outsourcer can set itself a goal for achieving a certain quality level (and therefore reward its executives) or to submit the data to the customer with the objective of obtaining new projects or of increasing the rate of payment for projects.

4.6 Cultural Differences

In any international business it is important to know the difference in thinking of people from various countries. That there are important perceptual differences among people from different cultures has been thoroughly documented and much has been written about the subject. Here we are going to touch on only those specific aspects that affect the process of outsourcing. People think differently, communicate differently, perceive things differently and respond to their managers differently. Some people may perceive something as being acceptable while others looking that the same thing deem it to be unacceptable. For example, an outsourcer was working in St. Petersburg and it was necessary that he find a picture for a presentation in the client's office in the United States. Wanting to show the cultural traditions of the city of St. Petersburg, the outsourcer chose the image of the Cathedral of the Savior of Spilled Blood, which is an architectural gem and which is not perceived by many people to be a religious structure. However, the customer issued strict instructions that there be "No church" in the picture. So, in the end, the outsourcer chose an image of a movable bridge that was an object of technology and that was still directly linked with the image of St. Petersburg.

There are certain problems inherent in the Russian mentality, such as if you need to get something from a Russian employee you will need to repeat the request three times. The logic behind this is that "if it is so important to you, dear boss, then why did you not remind me?" In Russia it is a good idea to agree after a request has been made three times. For example, if you visit someone and they offer you tea and cake the first answer would be: "Oh, no thanks, I just had something at home." A similar rule in England is that if you are offered home-made pastries, you should decline the first time but on the second offer you should take only one small pastry. In America, when offered tea you must immediately decide whether you want it or not. You will not be asked twice! Returning to specific examples in Russia, if there are multiple offers of cake then you should take some.

In America, even the most important instruction is given in the form of a soft, polite request. The imperative form of verbs is not used because that would be considered impolite. Instead of telling an American worker to "bring that over here," the supervisor would likely say "could you please bring that over here?" This latter form of speaking is very relaxing to a Russian who would not perceive that the task actually had to be done, even though in fact it is an order that must be carried out. Talking about polite language, we can't escape the temptation of quoting Winston Churchill's letter to Japan declaring the state of war following Japanese attack on Malaya, Singapore and Hong Kong. The letter was very ceremonial and polite, and it was signed: "I have the honour to be, with high consideration,

Sir, Your obedient servant, Winston S. Churchill"

In Russia, they do a great job of telling someone to do a job several times, roughly. If a boss is dissatisfied with an employee then he will tell him so several times in gruff language. If a boss reprimands and employee, even to the point of berating him, it does not mean that the boss hates the person. Instead, that kind of talk is probably common to the particular industry (like "shop jargon") and it could even mean that there is a friendly relationship between the parties. In an American company the employee might be requested to redo a task, but the request will be coached in softer terms and if the employee does not properly respond he will be fired, but also gently using the most politically correct terminology.

If you asked an American whether he liked your business proposal it is likely that he will answer "It's wonderful, thank you." However, this does not mean that the American thinks that the proposal is really good and that he will accept it. He is just being polite. In a similar way, consider the American smile. In the morning the American will have a smile on his face and never complain about anything. Russian programmers who have visited Americans on a business trip have said: "They're all so cheerful, so positive!" But, in reality, those smiles are just a form of being polite. Incidentally, the degree of friendliness varies with the different regions of the United States. In Texas it will be greater than in California and in California it is higher than in New York.

Russian outsourcing employees must remember that if they receive a letter or note from an American company saying that it is a "friendly reminder" then something is probably wrong and someone may be unhappy with the work. They must also remember not to use red text when writing to an American colleague because this is considered rude (emphasis should be blue, instead) and that writing in capital letters suggests aggression. Proposals should be written in a way that is sensitive to these issues.

In turn, employees of American companies operating in Russia should understand that what may seem to be crude from their point of view is not actually meant to be so. Rather it is a matter of different nuances in language and different notions of politeness.

Now, as more and more business processes are formalized and different tasks and reporting forms are standardized, all of these nuances and tones tend to be smoothed out. Older workers gradually become accustomed to dealing with them and the newer workers immediately adapt to the proper interpersonal format. However, just as the newcomers quickly assimilate into the contemporary culture, there is still a negative carryover from the old, traditional ways. For example, during his first two weeks an employee may report for work promptly at the scheduled time of 10:00 AM. But, then he begins to come in to work late, learning from the experience of other employees that he can probably get away with it. Of course, the manager has his own ways to ensure that employees begin work promptly and consistently as scheduled. But here it is necessary to consider another aspect of conducting international business that is the effect of time differences on conferences and late night telephone calls that take place with customers and whether in this case it is possible or practical to insist that the employee report to the office early. In any case, you need to monitor the behavior of employees. For example if an employee is required to have a late night telephone conference with a customer it could be reasonable that he not show up for work until lunch time. But, you do not want to see this situation persist and it is not that plausible that the same excuse is valid for two consecutive days. In this situation the problem may be solved by switching the time of the conference to the morning.

Every company has its own policy regarding attendance and punctuality. In general, exactly who or how many employees come into work is not that critical. What is most important is that the job is done in a timely and accurate manner. This is exactly the opposite of being criticized for being late – even by one minute!

When a manager gives and employee a wage increase in Russia everyone knows who received it and how much it was. In American it is exactly the opposite. Perhaps the roots of this Russian tradition comes from the Soviet Union, when salaries were published in a public document and before you told your family that you had received one, everyone else had the opportunity to know about it.

When interviewing potential candidates for a position an interviewer might ask: "Do you know such and such programming language?" Americans will say, "Yes, of course I know it. I am the best expert in this field." A Russian would answer, "I know a little," even if he is one of the world's top ten experts in field. Recently, the younger candidates have begun to learn to respond to questions like this in the "American style." But, in general the tendency to underestimate their skills remains and that must be borne in mind when hiring outsourcing company personnel.

During a conference call with its foreign partners, a Russian might say, "It is impossible to do this." But, he might really mean that he needs a more powerful computer to run the calculations. In fact, every problem has its solution and everything is possible. Here is an example. During a conference a Russian manager said that a problem could not be solved. In response, the U.S. customer stood up and slammed the door. In this case it was found that it was just necessary to make further efforts, which the Russian manager simply misstated, but the matter had to be referred to his boss. Another example is that when communicating with the customer in English do not use the word "difficult." Instead use the word "challenging." Both words translate into "difficult" in Russian but for an

American the first word suggests "impossible," while the second is "difficult but possible."

Of course, English is now considered the international language, but Americans will interpret a single meaning for a word while both Russians and the British see more than one meaning. Thus, for an American, the best word to describe a situation that has a difficult task to be performed is "problem." But, for the British it is "issue" and a Russian will not select a best word at all, he will just say that the task "is impossible to solve," notwithstanding that all things are possible with the right price.

It should be explained to Russian job seekers that letters from the outsourcing company must be answered within 24 hours. But, even if the issue is moot the recipient should respond with something like "I am undecided, I'll think about it." Unfortunately, the Russian practice is to either respond when they see fit or to not respond at all.

Russians often begin a phrase with the word "no" without there even being something to object to, i.e. "No, you know…" We must start with a "yes," even if there is there is an objection. Incidentally, the British start any conversation with a few sentences about the weather because this is the best way to agree with the speaker. "Today it is raining." "Oh yes, it is so damp." After several exchanges in which we agreed with each other we continued the dialogue on a positive note.

4.7 How to Send Employees on a Business Trip

In the early days of outsourcing the most important objective was to properly organize projects. If this had not been done then it would not have been possible to complete projects on time and at the best level of quality. In that case, the customer would not have been satisfied and outsourcing as a business would have ended before it really began. At that time, project management was fully dedicated to successfully complete a project. Customers remained happy and managers had few problems. Many years later project management became the simplest and best-established part of the work. But now there is another area that is causing problems – business travel.

Even experienced, adult employees can behave like children when they are in a foreign country. We would have to write a separate book to tell you all of the funny situations that have happened with our employees when they were on a business trip.

When we began this work we did not know how burdensome travel would be on an outsourcing company. But, our own employees and business colleagues have asked so many questions about organizing trips abroad that we decided to make the subject a separate chapter. The chapter explains how to travel from Russia to foreign countries and how to make a trip to Russia.

There are tons of simple rules which, if broken, can create many problems. It might seem that the rules are too obvious and that they need not be mentioned. However, many people do not follow the rules and continue to "step on a rake." We recommend that you read this chapter because despite the obvious, there is useful information that can help you avoid problems in your future travel.

So, if you are planning to travel we recommend that you remember the following:

1.   Make all payments by credit card.
2.   Do not use Russian airlines.
3.   Stay only in network (chain) hotels.

4.8. Credit Cards

4.8.1. The History of Credit Cards

Let's start with the historical perspective. In ancient times carrying a lot of money meant that a person had to carry a heavy bag of coins. This was both inconvenient and dangerous. Later travelers carried "letters of credit" that they gave to a banker to obtain cash. These letters date back to early times and have been described in many historical novels, in particular in "The Count of Monte Cristo." In 1772 the first traveler's checks were issued by the London Credit Exchange Company and in 1874 Thomas Cook began issuing "circular notes" to facilitate the exchange of credit during travel. However, somewhat later the president of the American Express Company (then a postal business) was traveling in Europe and discovered that this type of instrument was useful only in large cities. He was quite unhappy to learn that he could not obtain cash in smaller towns. So, American Express started developing a widespread traveler's check system which was introduced in 1991.

Later, American Express ceased to be a postal company when it involuntarily sold its network of railroads to the government. The company retained its financial businesses, however and made a fortune in bank cards. However, the credit card was not invented by American Express. The invention of credit cards took place in the twentieth century. Until that time, it was easy to obtain credit in the small shops of towns and villages and, for that matter, in the local shops in larger cities. Everyone lived in the same neighborhood and everyone knew each other. Then, as U.S. business developed, the larger stores made obtaining goods on credit easy. Large retail chains like Sears Roebuck & Co. and Montgomery Ward believed that every person was entitled to credit so they issued their own credit cards. Gas station chains quickly joined in this practice.

The next stage in the development of credit cards occurred in New York. A man named Frank McNamara went to an expensive restaurant, dined and found out that he did not have sufficient cash to pay the bill. Frank decided that there must be an alternative to cash to pay for meals at a restaurant and invented a credit card called Diner's Club. The Diner's Club cards became very popular, but they could be used only to pay for meals at restaurants – nothing more.

The idea of a universal credit card that would pay for all goods and services can be traced to the end of the nineteenth century. At that time American author Edward Bellamy, in his fictional novel "Looking Back" that was published in 1888, described American society in the twentieth century. In this society there was a cult of consumption, but there was no money. Instead, credit cards were used for the purchase of goods.

The first truly universal credit card was introduced in California in the 1950s when the Bank of America issued its "BankAmericard." The logo on the card consisted of three colored stripes, blue, white and golden-brown (the color of California and its hills). Eventually, the card was called "Visa," retaining the same logo. In the beginning, these cards were handed out indiscriminately. They became so popular that it was frightening and it caused the Bank of America a financial crisis because 22 percent of the people who used the cards did not pay their credit card bill when it became due. After this event, the person who was responsible for designing the credit card was fired and the cards were thereafter distributed only after it was determined that a card holder had the ability to pay his bills. In order to distribute the cards outside of California it was necessary to allow other banks to have the right to issue the same card. Another credit card that became popular during this period was the American Express card, but unlike Visa, American Express is not issued by other financial institutions and remains a "closed system."

A few years later, in order to compete with Visa, a group of other banks released the "Master Charge," later renamed "Master Card."

In the 1980s still another credit card arose in the United States, the Discover card. The unique feature of this card was that instead of being charged a fee for the privilege of using the card, holders of the Discover card received a cash bonus when they use it to pay for something. This enabled the Discover card to become popular very quickly. However, other credit card companies realized that a bonus system was a good way to capture market share and today that has become a common practice.

4.8.2 Credit versus Debit Cards

Here is how a credit card differs from a debit card: a credit card allows you to spend someone else's money (the money of the bank) with the understanding that you have incurred a debt and must reimburse the bank for the money that it advanced to the merchant on your behalf. When you use a debit card you are actually spending your own money. Credit cards require repayment, either in a single repayment or in periodic payments such as once per month. Interest is usually charged to the card holder if payment is made in installments, but not when the credit card holder pays off the card balance in full upon receipt of the bill.

When a person buys something and pays for it with a "Card" he is asked whether it is "debit" or "credit." This means that the person must choose between two methods of payment. If the person chooses to pay via credit card then he is asked to sign for the payment, except that some merchants do not require a signature if the sales amount is small, like under $50.00. But, if payment is made via debit card then the purchaser will be asked to enter a PIN (Personal Identification Number). The end result is much the same. The purchaser does not have to pay cash directly to the merchant; the transfer of funds is handled by the card holder's bank. Interestingly however, when a debit card is used the merchant might ask the purchaser if he would like any "cash back." For example, the actual purchase amount might be $25.00 but the purchaser (card holder) asks for $25.00 cash back. In that case the merchant processes the sale, gives the purchaser $25.00 in cash and then records a total transaction amount of $50.00, which is debited by the card holder's bank from his bank account. So, in a real sense, the merchant is playing the role of an ATM. Remember, cash can only be obtained when a debit card is used, except for the Discover Card, which was discussed earlier. Cash cannot be obtained this way when a credit card is used.

In Russia, bank cards are universally referred to as "credit cards." But, in fact, they are really not credit cards but rather debit cards. The traveler might encounter a situation in which he sees something that he wants to purchase and the Visa symbol and logo are displayed in the store and at the checkout counter. However, at checkout when the customer gives the cashier his credit card the cashier asks for the PIN code. Unfortunately, many people do not remember their PIN code for their credit card because it is usually not needed. The buyer will tell the cashier that he needs to record "credit" with the signature, but the cashier is not familiar with that protocol because his management only instructed him how to process debit cards. The traveler might need a lot of cash to deal with situations like that.

In general, in Russia there are both humorous and sad stories about the use of both credit and debit cards. We remember one day in late 1999 when we were refused the use of a credit card in a restaurant because it was almost New Year and at that time there was much concern about the Millennium Crash that would cause a failure in the bank's electronic network. Of course, that did not happen.

There are some advantages of using a credit card that are not shared with the use of either cash or a debit card. Some of these are important to the person who is traveling away from home. Using a credit card is also a form of consumer protection. If the purchaser alleges that the seller sold him defective goods or that a substandard service was rendered, he can dispute the transaction and the burden of proof that the purchaser's claim is not true falls on the seller. This is an excellent form of consumer protection for purchasing goods, buying airline tickets, staying at a hotel, or renting a car and much more. For example, suppose that you purchase airline tickets using your credit card and the airline goes into bankruptcy. In that case the bank will refund the money that you paid for the tickets.

Lost or stolen credit cards can be quickly restored. For example, American Express has offices all over the world. If the holder of an American Express card loses his card he can go to any American Express office, obtain cash on the spot and have the card immediately reissued.

There are two stages to the processing of credit card transactions. The first is the actual transaction such as the purchase of goods and the second is the confirmation of the purchase. When the transaction is processed by the card company, an equivalent amount is "frozen" against the card holder's account. The card holder is not inconvenienced by this process as the "frozen" amount is not recorded on its balance sheet. But, if a debit card is used, the amount of the transaction is "frozen" against the card holder's bank account until the card holder's bank "unfreezes" it. This problem is best illustrated when a card holder is traveling. For example, if a card holder stays at a hotel, the hotel will usually "freeze" a certain amount against the person's account in case the guest uses the mini-bar or telephone or other of the amenities of the hotel for which a fee is charged. In the case of a debit card, that amount will not be "unfrozen" until the bank issuing the card "unfreezes" them, but that can take a week or a month or more.

One additional benefit of some credit cards is that they provide a certain amount of insurance when the card holder rents a car. In many cases this insurance is less costly than the insurance that is available directly from the car rental agency. Depending on the particular credit card used, this insurance might be free or it might be offered at nominal cost, like $18.00 for a 45 day car rental, which works out to be only 40 cents per day. The e3xtent of these additional benefits is often determined by the level of the card holder's card, i.e. Silver, Gold or Platinum level, etc. In any case, these are all desirable features of credit cards.

In this chapter we have presented only some of the features of credit cards, which in our opinion are very important for travel. Debit cards usually do not provide these features, although in outward appearance they may seem to be indistinguishable from credit cards. This is due to the fact that credit card companies charge a much higher fee for processing transactions and therefore can afford to fund the additional services that they offer.

We need to explain an important difference among the various types of bank cards. There are closed bank card systems, like American Express, which until very recently are issued only by a single company – the American Express Company. In recent years, under competitive pressure, American Express has been allowing some banks to issue American Express cards under their name.

There are also "open system" bank cards, like Visa and MasterCard, which are widely issued by different banks under their own name. This is a very competitive system and until recently banks were allowed to issue more than one type of bank card (either credit or debit). Now there are certain limitations to this practice. Visa is more popular in Europe that MasterCard, while this is reversed somewhat in the U.S.

Theoretically, the merchant does not have the right to ask for the buyer's identification when the buyer uses MasterCard (this is usually ignored in Russia), but requiring documentation is not prohibited when using Visa. Still, a lack of identification is not proper grounds for refusal to honor either card.

In Europe and the U.S., a person can rent a car and either use his personal credit card for payment or he can use a corporate card that is based on special terms and conditions negotiated between his employer and the car rental company or, in some cases, no card is needed at all because funds will be transferred directly from the employer to the car rental agency. If there is no such agreement then a credit or debit card will definitely be needed. However, bank cards issued in Russia will generally not be accepted even if they are part of the international card system network.

As a further measure of consumer protection, the issuers of the major credit cards have a system that tracks exactly how much money is spent. If there are dubious credit card transactions (such as purchases in questionable places, for example) the bank will usually call the credit card holder and ask if everything is in order. In a "worst case" situation the money in the account may be blocked to prevent fraudulent transfer of funds. This system is the reason why credit card transactions in Russia are often declined by the bank. If the seller is knowledgeable about this system he can save a response code and the customer can call the bank to authorize the transaction. But, in most cases the employee processing the transaction does not understand how this system works and simply informs the card holder that the transaction could not be processed. He then apologizes and returns the card to the customer. Because of this, it is recommended that anyone traveling from the U.S. to "questionable locations," like Russia or Mexico, call their bank and inform it of the upcoming trip. The restriction will then usually be lifted. If the customer has already purchased airline tickets to the country in question then all of this is generally not a problem because the bank can verify the travel destination of the customer.

In Russia not all ATMs participate in the international system. Therefore, even if the ATM carries the Visa logo it does not mean that the ATM will give money when an American Visa card is used.

Traditionally, in Europe credit cards are less common than in the U.S. Some people believe that the bank card is an element of total state control over the actions of its citizens because purchases can be tracked and indicate the behavioral pattern of the card holder. Today more and more Europeans and Americans are worried that "Big Brother" will be following them.

4.9. How to Get a Visa

Entry visas that allow foreigners to enter a country emerged in the twentieth century as a result of the massive displacement of people across borders in World War I. European countries, wanting to control this movement, imposed visa restrictions. In 1924 the United States also began requiring entry visas.

Since then the system has been repeatedly changed and different countries have changed it in various ways. In general, the greatest number of visa restrictions occurred during the Cold War between the West and the Soviet Union. But now, almost one hundred years after World War I, the world is striving to achieve visa free entry. This is because the concept of a visa being an instrument to control illegal immigration is obsolete for two reasons. First, economic globalization has significantly decreased migration flows between countries. Secondly, governments have more effective control over the movement of undesirable people than by requiring visas.

The world is still only in the early stages of abolishing visas, so when someone goes on a business trip he will likely still need to carry a business visa. Citizens of the U.S., EU and the UK can enjoy visa-free entry into a number of countries. The most fortunate in this respect are the British who can visit 174 countries around the world without the need for a visa. However, most of the more popular outsourcing countries – India, China and Russia – require visas for citizens of the United States and the European Union. Russians have less to worry about then most of the others. As a consolation to Russian readers, we note that there are countries in which Americans need a visa but Russians do not, for example Brazil.

The procedures for obtaining a visa range from light to burdensome. One of the most burdensome is the Japanese procedure for obtaining a business visa because it requires a lot of documents supplied not by the person for whom the visa is intended but rather from the organization of the host country. For example, the company inviting the employee on the business trip must submit a statement that it has no debts, is properly registered and the invited person must submit his passport. But, the company must also send the invitation written in Japanese. This is a problem because it is difficult to translate the document and secondly, by rules of etiquette, the composition of the document must be in "flowery" Eastern terminology that is so complex that it is sometimes impossible to understand the "who, when, where and for how long" aspects of the visa application.

Each country has certain roles about what activities are permissible for the person who enters the country on a business visa. The most extensive list of permitted activities is found in South Korea, which allows a business person to engage in market research, advisory services, the execution of a contract, the installation and debugging of software and training. Italy has the most restrictive list. There a person with a business visa is practically restricted from engaging in any business activity except for three things: conducting business meetings, searching for partners to enter into a business contract, and diagnosing a problem with either hardware or software that the person's company has shipped to Italy. Interestingly, repairing the hardware or software after diagnosis is not permitted. For example, if a software developer discovers a bug in the code it would be illegal to correct the problem on site by a representative who is in Italy on a business visa.

A visitor to the U.S. who holds a type B1 business visa has the right to conduct a business meeting, participate in scientific or educational conferences and symposia and may participate in court proceedings as either a defendant or plaintiff. Also, under a business visa a visitor to the U.S. has the right to participate in commercial transactions not involving employment, i.e. he can sign a contract but not actually perform work. The holder of a U.S. type B1 visa can also bring product samples into the country, look for business partners and has the right to service equipment or software brought into the country within one year of the sales transaction. The holder of a U.S. type B2 tourist visa also has the right to engage in some commercial activities. For example, if a foreigner entered the U.S. on a tourist visa and then returned to his home in another country, he has the right to re-enter the U.S. on that tourist visa (if it is still valid at the time) and conduct some business affairs. But, there are limitations to this; for example, the person could not conduct lectures for which a type J1 visa would be required. In general, U.S. visa laws are confusing.

Russia, by contrast, does not allow the holders of tourist visas to engage in business affairs. However, many people ignore this rule and have found a way around it. It is easier to obtain a tourist visa to enter Russia than a business visa. So, one common way around the problem is to book a room in a major Russian hotel. The hotel sends the person a fax confirming the reservation, which is sufficient to obtain a tourist visa. Traditionally, a reservation is made at the hotel Cosmos in St. Petersburg – in the "Pulkovo." Note that this hotel is not recommended as the real place of lodging for visitors from the West because its services and amenities remain at the level to which they declined during the period of socialism in Russia.

Returning to the subject of the Russian business visas, the list of permitted work activities is quite extensive and reasonable. A person can enter into contracts, carry out installation and maintenance of software, check on product quality, purchase products, attend lectures, and conduct training sessions. (Note, the right to conduct a lecture on a business visa is permitted when there is an absence of domestic expertise on the subject.)

Most countries allow a visa holder to remain in their country for 90 consecutive days, although the duration of the visa, itself, might be much longer, like 6 months to a year. The U.S. allows visa holders to remain in its territories for up to six months.

According to Russian law, if a person lived abroad for more than 90 days and then returns to take residency in Russia, his taxes will increase sharply. A person who lives for more than 90 days in California is subject to paying California state taxes. This problem is often faced by pilots who have to calculate exactly how much they were in the air over the state of California.

4.9.1 Are You a Terrorist? Features of the Visa in the U.S.

A U.S. visa is one of the most difficult visas to obtain. At the same time, it is one of the most desirable. Because of this it is important to understand under what conditions it is granted or refused. One task confronting the visa applicant is to convince the U.S. Consul that they are not even thinking of staying in the U.S. illegally.

We had the chance to speak with the U.S. Consul in Russia. The consul said that the number one criterion for obtaining a visa to the U.S. is for the applicant to have a long-term, well-paying job by local standards. In a situation where an employer has hired a new employee who the employer wants to send to the U.S., the U.S. consulate will review that person's previous work experience. If, for example, a person previously worked as a waiter then suddenly became CEO of the company the visa will most likely be denied to him.

The second most important criterion regarding the issuance of a visa to the United States is whether the person has previously traveled to the West, including all of Europe except Finland. We assume that this is because a

Finnish visa is relatively easy to obtain.

The third point that the Consul indicated was the presence of spouses or children that remain in the home country while the person is traveling. Traditionally, the presence of "hostages" in Russia has been viewed as a positive criterion for the issuance of a U.S. visa. However, the consul stated that now it is considered either a neutral or even a negative factor. There is no logic behind this. It is strictly based on statistics, sometimes people who have family in Russia remain in the U.S. and work there illegally. Apparently there are fewer and fewer people who are considered "hostages" in Russia. If you have relatives in the U.S. it actually reduces your chances of obtaining a U.S. visa since the Consul thinks that the relatives will help the person stay in the U.S. illegally.

The occupation of the visa applicant has a bearing on the amount of time it takes to obtain a U.S. visa. The American consulate is positively biased toward physicists in certain areas of specialization and in those cases processes applications in just a few months. If an applicant is told that his case is being discussed in Washington and that he must wait for two months then that is a good sign. If the consul intended to deny the application he would have done so immediately and would not have bothered with using a delaying technique such as saying that the application was being considered in Washington. Usually in such cases the decision will be positive.

The above mentioned Consul shared humorous stories about his experience with visa applicants. On the visa application there was the following question: "Are you a terrorist?" In one case the applicant wrote "Yes." This caused the people in the consulate to run around in panic as they feared that the person was a suicide bomber. But, in reality the problem was a matter of emotion, short-sightedness or a poor understanding of the English language. The applicant misunderstood the word "terrorist" and thought that it was "tourist," instead.

According to the U.S. consul, U.S. officials check to determine whether the stated purpose of the travel to the U.S. is permissible. For example, suppose that an outsourcer travels to the U.S. on a B1 visa but instead of participating in production meetings or study (which is allowable) he begins to work as a software developer. This is not permissible and the consulate will consider it to be a blatant violation. In such case, it will punish not only the offender but also the sponsoring company by, for example, ceasing to issue visas to any of that outsourcing company's employees and possibly by levying heavy fines against the host American company.

Since outsourcing is now well-established in America, a new type of visa called "B1 in lieu of H1" has been created in addition to the former H1 visa. The purpose for this new type of visa is to permit employees of large, well-established foreign companies to enter the U.S. and carry on business activities within its territories for up to one year. The visa holder must be an employee of the foreign company which must be responsible for paying for his work. Prior to the B1 in lieu of H1visa, it was necessary for a person to obtain n H1 visa that required the person to actually become an employee of the American company, or an L1 in the case of an American headquartered multi-national company.

4.9.2 Getting a Russian Visa

In Russia there is a Stalin Era song in which one line states: "There is no other country I know where a man can breathe so freely." Of course, while in such a country obtaining a visa should be just a cinch; but in reality you cannot let just anyone breathe that freely.

Applying for a visa is a thankless task. In the old language style we would say that visa regulations are changing so fast that new ones are issued even before the ink is dry on the old ones. In modern style we would rather say something like trying to keep up with the new iPhone models. This is doubly true for Russian visa rules.

The history of Russian visa rules sometimes takes surprising forms. We cannot help but quote the historical document: "Allow the KGB (then known as OGPU) the passage of foreigners with visas, expired no more than 15 days ago" (From the minutes of the Politbureau meeting number 116, a special folder, 1932). Now it is impossible to suggest even in theory that the country would have allowed the use of expired visas.

In order to obtain a visa to Russia you need an official invitation from a Russian company. The company, therefore, must be a specially registered participant of foreign economic activity. Just a letter confirming the purpose of the trip is not enough; the invitation must be on official letterhead and bear the company seal. It is possible that the invitation will be issued by a third party that is an agency specializing in this kind of activity that is being paid by the inviting company. It will take several days for the recipient to receive this invitation in the case of a single entry visa and up to several weeks for multiple entry visas. An original copy of the invitation will have to be presented to the consulate either in person or by Express Mail.

In making a visa application, a copy of the passport of the traveling person is required. The application must include the passport number, date and place and purpose of the trip. The entire process of the invitation and its delivery takes time. It may happen that the passport that the traveler submits to the Russian consulate is not the same passport that was used to issue the invitation. For example, while waiting for an invitation perhaps an old passport was replaced by a new one. Or, it is possible that the U.S. person has two passports that are valid for different reasons (perhaps dual citizenship) and that different ones were used for the visa and invitation. This is not an issue and the Russian consulate will issue a visa anyway.

The minimum term for a business visa is two weeks and the maximum term is one year. There are also special invitations for a three year multi-visa (in and out of Russia). While it is theoretically possible to obtain a three year multi-visa, the system for issuing one in Russia has not yet been established and there are no clear procedures for obtaining the required invitation.

In order to avoid wasting time and energy waiting for a business visa to be issued, businessmen traveling to Russia often enter using a tourist visa. Naturally, they do not go to museums or other tourist places. As law-abiding people, Americans are uncomfortable with these situations and frankly prefer to obtain a visa that corresponds with the real purpose of the trip.

There is an awkward aspect of obtaining a visa for travel to Russia for third-world nationals who are living in the United States. Russia demands that a passport be valid for six months after the passport expiration date. This is a common requirement and many countries honor it. A foreign national residing in the United States is likely to have a "green card" or a visa for entry into the United States (e.g. H1). For the duration of the passport period, the Russian consulate requires that the green card or visa also be valid for a period of six months after the person files an application for a visa for entry into Russia. This is an unusual requirement. If the green card or visa is not valid for that period then the consulate will not issue a visa. Instead, it will recommend that the person who is applying return to his native country and make a visa application from there.

What happens if you lose your passport while on a trip to Russia? The Consulate General of your country will likely give you a new passport quickly. The U.S. Consulate General has two options to issue you a new one. If you have an important reason to return immediately, you will be issues a passport which is valid for three month. It will take about 15 minutes for the US Consulate to issue such passport. If you can wait for a few days, then you will get a normal US passport being valid for ten years (five for children). However, you will not be able to leave Russia with the new passport. The new passport will not have a Russian visa attached with it and you will not be allowed to leave. You will first have to obtain a duplicate visa with the new passport, which will take one week, and only then will you be allowed to leave Russia. The process of obtaining a duplicate visa is so bureaucratic and time consuming, so you may decide never travel to Russia again. We recommend asking the US Consulate for a list of local service providers that can help you with this matter.

At the time of this book publication, a new set of Russian Visa rules got into effect. In accordance with the new agreement between the Russian Federation and the United States of America on the simplification of visa formalities for nationals of the Russian Federation and nationals of the United States of America the US citizens shall as a rule be issued multiple-entry business, private, humanitarian and tourist visas for a stay of no more than 6 months starting from the date of each entry that are valid for three years (36 months) from the date of issue of the visa. The new Visa rules did not invalidate the old ones. You can apply for a Visa either way. The new rules have definite advantages: you no longer need an invitation from Russian authorities; instead a letter from the inviting company is enough. The letter can be sent via email and printed locally. If you enter Russia with the new style Visa, lose your passport, and get a new passport replacement then the reincarnation of the Russian entry Visa no longer required to exit the country. This is a good step reducing troubles and headache.

Before being granted a visa for entry in to Russia, former citizens of the Soviet Union must prove that they are not now citizens of the USSR. Even if the person has lived in American for many years, he must still provide documents that prove exactly how he went from the USSR to America. Of course, most people do not keep documents for that long so there have been cases where a visa was denied because of lack of proper documentation. In recent years the situation has changed and the Russian consulate has accepted a letter explaining that the documents were lost. Also, if a person became a U.S. citizen in 1996 or earlier, that is sufficient proof that the person is no longer a Russian citizen. Here is the rationale for that policy. The Russian consulate believes that it took a former citizen of the Soviet Union five years from the time that he entered the country before U.S. Immigration approved his application for U.S. citizenship. Thus, the consulate believes that if a person obtained U.S. citizenship in 1996 he had to emigrate to the U.S. in 1991 or earlier. At that time the former USSR deprived a person of citizenship if that person left to take up permanent residency in another country. Thus, in the opinion of the Consulate of Russia, this proves that the person who received U.S. citizenship in 1996 or earlier could not have retained citizenship in Russia, as the successor to the Soviet Union. Surprisingly, the "1996 threshold year" may differ from Consulate to Consulate within US. The logic behind the variations is unknown. We recommend double-checking with the local Russian Consulate.

Apparently, this situation with visas for former citizens of the USSR is due to the fact that Russia is putting pressure on its former citizens to reclaim their citizenship back to report an increase in Russian population. Presently the population in Russia is declining.

4.10 How to Miss a Flight

There is a secret known by all experienced air travelers. What do you do if you arrive for your flight late? There are many reasons why this might happen. There might be an extra-long line at the check-in counter or at airport security. Perhaps there was a traffic jam or you could not find a place to park. In any event, you get to the gate too late. What do you do next? Of course you ask the airline to put you on another flight. But, the secret is that the airline will reschedule you to the next flight FREE – of extra charge, even if your ticket rules requires a fee for change! The reason for your being late does not matter. Western airlines (American and European) are fighting to get customers and will do anything to keep customers happy. The airlines have found that it is more profitable to put you on the next available flight and send you to your destination at no additional cost than to lose you to the competition. In this case your loyalty to the airline will increase and you will stop using other competing airlines. Russians usually do not believe in getting flight change for free. When we wrote about this secret in a Russian Internet media, we received comments like that: "What a stupid idea! You, guys, apparently never took a flight!"

There is another aspect to this secret in Russia. First, Russian airlines are not as interested in their customers' satisfaction and will require extra payment in case of a missed flight. You have no alternative to avoid this except to not use Russian airlines. Never! Simply do not fly on them. Secondly, the Russian officials of foreign companies are not even aware of the existence of this secret. It is useless to even discuss it with the employees of foreign airlines with offices in Russia. The secret is to immediately call the central reservations office of the airline company in the U.S. For example, if you arrived late for a Delta Airlines flight from Moscow to New York, call the central reservations office of Delta in Atlanta. They will gladly arrange to put you on the next available flight and you will soon be on your way!

Here is another situation. Your airline delays your flight or cancels it altogether and you are late for the change to the next flight. The airline, of course, offers to schedule you on yet another flight on which there are seats available. Well, if the flights are frequent you might lose only a few hours. But what do you do if the delay or changeover would be a day or more? This does happen, but rarely. The simplest solution is to ask the airline staff to route you through a different point of transfer to your destination. That way you may lose a few hours but not an entire day or more. It is even more effective to ask the airline on which your flight is booked to send you to your destination on another airline using the same ticket. Do not hesitate to request this! U.S. airlines are very willing to "pick up" foreign passengers in this situation because they understand that this way they will acquire a very long-term and loyal customer base. If there are seats available you are sure to be put on a flight of a competitor. No additional fee is charged in this case!

Sometimes you purchase a ticket that involves several stops and layovers with flight segments that are on different airlines. In this case even a small delay can cause you to miss a connecting flight. In the event of a tight connection, you should ask the airline on which you are traveling to arrange for a more speedy transfer to the next gate or to the other terminal for you. In some cases the airline will arrange for a car to be waiting at the tarmac to take you to the next gate for the continuation of your flight.

Think ahead when planning for your next trip. Decide in advance what you will do if certain situations arise. Check to see if there are alternate flights that can get you to your destination. For example, if you fly Delta airlines from San Francisco to Moscow with a change in New York and the flight to New York is late (causing you to miss the New York to Moscow flight) then there are two more opportunities to fly to Moscow the same day. There is an Aeroflot flight that usually leaves New York two hours after the Delta flight and then there is an Air France flight that would route you through Paris to Moscow.

Sometimes passengers whose flights are delayed are stuck at the point of transfer and are forced to spend the entire night there. Western airlines usually pay for the hotel and dinner in that case. You should consider how you will spend your time if this happens during your flight. For example, if you are flying from Moscow to San Francisco there are more interesting things to do in New York than in Atlanta, or in Paris rather than in Frankfurt. But, what do you do if you are flying to/from the U.S and there is a long delay in the connecting flight in Europe but you do not have the proper visa? Simply ask the airline employees to help you get a one-day visa to enter the city. As a rule, in such cases one-day visas are quick and easy to get.

When planning for your trip you have to decide what to take with you. Should you check baggage or just take "carry-on" luggage. There is limited carry-on space on most airplanes. There are pros and cons for each alternative. If you check baggage then it is possible that your luggage will be on the next flight segment before you are. If you are transferring to another terminal the airplane for your next flight will be waiting for you. If your luggage is aboard but you cannot make the flight the airplane will not be permitted to leave the gate without you. So, the airline will be forced to identify your luggage and remove it from the plane before it can depart. Unloading your staff can take some time. Experienced travelers have learned to take advantage of this. It makes sense to check in a piece of luggage if you have a tight connection. You will have some extra time to make the flight because the airline will wait few minutes before start indentifying and unloading your luggage.

On the other hand, if you have all of your belongings with you in a carry-on the plane will not wait for you. Again, experienced travelers have learned to take advantage of this situation as well. Imagine that upon arrival in Paris you must transfer to another airline, in another terminal, and that the connection time is only 45 minutes. Well, you should go very slowly. Buy a Coke, perhaps, and drink it slowly or do something else that take up time. As a result, your original flight leaves without you. But, the airline schedules you for another flight. This is exactly what you want! You now have several hours to tour the beautiful city. In only a half-hour you can get to the Paris North Station by train, and enjoy the city for a few hours!

4.11 How to Survive a Business Trip to Russia

Imagine that you are traveling to Russia for the first time. In this chapter we will give you some tips that are usually not included in tourist guides. The tips will help to make you feel more comfortable during your time in Russia.

4.11.1 Renting a Car

If you are thinking about renting a car – think again. The problem of traffic congestion in both Moscow and St. Petersburg is so great that it has a strong effect on both business and personal life. You cannot make an appointment on time if you try to get there by car. At least there is a chance that you will make the appointment if you hire a car with driver or take a taxi. That way you can always get out of the car and take the subway. But if you drive a car yourself you cannot escape and you will be left stuck in traffic wasting a lot of time. There are other problems associated with renting a car also, but these can be overcome – in contrast to the traffic for which there is no solution. For example, in the event of an accident the driver is prohibited from leaving the scene and will have to spend half a day waiting for the police to arrive and issue documents. Also, Russia does not recognize the national driver's license of other countries – only international drivers' permits.

When renting a car there is a high probability that you will be given an old car and that it might break. Typically, it takes about three days to get a replacement vehicle. You should be prepared to use other methods of transportation during that period. Once a traveler got a rental car at the Moscow airport. Upon reaching the center of Moscow he discovered that the clutch (it was a manual transmission) malfunctioned. The car came to a dead standstill in the middle of the street. The rental agency (it was SIXT) took the car in for repair, but refused to replace it with another one and required the traveler to pay for the repair of the clutch. The rental agency believed that the traveler was from the United States where all cars have automatic transmissions and that he broke the clutch because of lack of skill using a stick shift. It was Friday night. On Monday morning the traveler called the SIXT headquarter in Germany and made a complaint. In a half hour he received a call from the Moscow branch of telling him that people were coming to him with their apologies. Since then the traveler only travels around Moscow in a car with driver.

4.11.2 Currency Exchange

The Russian Federation has recently enacted a prohibition of private currency exchange offices. Now all currency exchange transactions must be made at the offices of banks or their branches. Before this currency exchange offices were located most anywhere – even in a little nook in a basement that looked more like a hangout of the Mafia. Now the situation has improved and the exchange offices look more decent. In Russia, the difference between the buying and selling exchange rates has traditionally been small. This is because people in Russia often change their rubles into foreign currency and vise-versa, while in many other countries this service is targeted only at tourists. The preferred method of getting cash is the ATM, where it is easier to use a debit card rather than a credit card. The ATM will rarely allow anyone to withdraw more than the equivalent of $200.00 in rubles. The ATM fee could be more than five dollars, but the exchange rate is often better than in the exchange offices. In airport arrival terminals, there are often both exchange offices and ATMs located in the customs area. However, you should be warned, it is better not to use them. The exchange rates in these areas will not be in your favor. There are other ATMs with much better exchange rates located immediately outside the Exit from the customs area. The difference could exceed 15% in the traveler's favor.

When exchanging currency keep in mind that in Russia there are restrictions on the export of money in cash form. It is generally recommended that upon departure you should not have more than $10,000.00 per family in rubles and foreign currencies in total. At the time this book was written currency exchange offices were banned after passing departure control (although they were permitted earlier). So, exchange your remaining rubles before crossing customs.

4.11.3 Taxi

At the time that this was written, there was no organized system of taxi service at the arrival area of the airports. After exiting the customs terminal travelers were besieged by strange people who offered (sometimes aggressively) a taxi ride into the city. We strongly recommend that you use the service of official taxi drivers who will charge one-third the rate of the "gypsy" taxis. It is best to arrange for a taxi in advance –even before your flight – by calling ahead to a private service. Request that the driver hold a sign at the exit from customs. By the way, the sign does not necessarily show your name; it can be written in a code word or the name of the company. When you call for a taxi remember that in Russia they speak Russian and not much English, so use a Russian speaking person when calling a dispatcher. We recommend that you give the taxi service your flight number so that if your plane is late the taxi cab company employees will understand what is happening (where the client disappeared to). The cars used as taxis in Russia are very different from in many other countries. You may pay little money for a decent car but at the same time you might wind up with an old, smoky clunker. When you order a taxi specify that it is for business. It may be a little more expensive but the car will be better.

When ordering a taxi, if you have a cell phone (and someone who speaks Russian) give the number to the taxi company. Then the taxi driver will call you to let you know that he has arrived and is waiting for you. In Russia taxi drivers rarely help to put things in the trunk or take them out. If the weather is wet or if the asphalt is dirty do not let the driver put your luggage down. He might put it in the mud or a puddle. When you become accustomed to the harsh realities of the Russian driver you will learn to not draw attention to the situation but instead simply handle your own baggage.

Once we ordered a car with a driver to pick up an important visitor from the United States. We asked the agency to make sure that the driver would help with the baggage, not smoke and not talk too much and wear a suit. We were told that the agency would take care of everything except that they could not make the driver wear a suit. It is unrealistic to expect a driver to wear a suit in Russia.

In Moscow, in contrast to many other places in the world, the cost of a taxi is not only based on mileage but also on travel time because of the traffic jams.

4.11.4 Hotels

Russian hotel chains are not as extensive as in the West, but in general the industry is well developed. You can locate and book a hotel through the Internet. We recommend that when traveling to Russia foreigners stay in hotels that are part of a chain or network where the quality of service will be at the highest level. The range of hotels is sufficiently ample – from luxury to inexpensive hostels. Mini-hotels are very common in St. Petersburg, but if the hotel is small it does not mean that it is necessarily inexpensive. You should check the price of a hotel carefully.

Imagine that the hotel is booked for a certain dollar amount per night but that it was not paid for in advance. In that case the traveler might get a surprise when paying upon checkout. The hotel will not disregard the price in dollars that was set at the time of booking. However, the actual payment will be calculated in rubles and the hotel will apply its own "hotel rate of exchange," which might differ greatly from the current bank exchange rate. As a result, the traveler will pay 10% to 15% more than was indicated at the time of booking. Our recommendation is to prepay for lodging with a major credit card issued by a U.S. bank. The bank will side with the traveler in case there is a dispute.

Some hotels include breakfast, which is usually very expensive if paid separately. If breakfast is not included it can be easy and pleasant to have breakfast in a café outside of the hotel. In the past, Russian hotels did not offer breakfast. But now it has become a common practice.

4.11.5 Metro

There are some things that foreign travelers must remember when coming to Russia. In Moscow taking photos in the subway is prohibited. In St. Petersburg taking photos in the subway is allowed but only without using a flash.

Finding your way around the Moscow subway system is difficult but not nearly as hopeless as in London or Paris. In St. Petersburg, there are markings in color and station names are duplicated in Latin.

4.11.6 Restaurants

As a general rule, do not go to restaurants that do not accept credit cards, except for restaurants that the "locals" recommend. Many restaurants seem to be extremely expensive and at the same time they are half empty, except for the inevitable few from the fashion circuit. Price usually has nothing to do with quality. The absence of a crowd does not always mean that the food in that restaurant is bad. Rather, the business model of the restaurant might be designed to accommodate fewer people at any particular time. For example, in a small restaurant in St. Petersburg called the "Coffee House," the waitress will warn you that service will be slow because there are a lot of restaurant patrons, even though you can see that more than half the tables are not occupied.

For the most part, slow service is a "typical disease" of Russian restaurants. Moreover, the more expensive the restaurant the slower is the service. This is because in the more expensive restaurants meals are prepared individually once you have ordered everything. In such restaurants there are no pre-cooked ingredients. In Russia, the words "prepared individually" mean that the entire meal is prepared from scratch. If the meal includes meat then be assured that in the kitchen they take raw meat and begin to prepare it only after you have placed your order. Therefore, when ordering a meal be sure to ask how long it will take to prepare it.

Finding vegetarian dishes in Russian restaurants might be something of a problem. If you have a guest from abroad who is a vegetarian you will have to call the restaurant where you plan on dining (or better yet go there) and learn if they can accommodate the guest's desires. In many cases restaurants in Russia will agree to prepare vegetarian dishes for you if you negotiate this in advance with them. In Russia, even in the most elegant restaurants there are business lunches. The price of these lunches is not great and they give you an opportunity to dine in a very nice environment without "breaking" your monthly budget.

4.11.7 Return Flight

In some of Russia's older airports the customs inspection occurs before you actually check in for the flight. Most people go through a "green corridor" in which there is no customs inspection and no one is stopped. In the newer airports, the order matches the European style: Check-in – Customs - Passport Control - Security Control – Boarding.

Expect a long line at passport control. Many passengers begin to worry that they will be late for their flight. However, if you are traveling on a Western airline the pilot is usually aware of delays at passport control and will hold the plane for the passengers.

If you want to depart on a flight other than the one specified on your ticket then you can register for stand-by status. This means that space might not yet be available but the airline has reason to believe that a seat will become available before the flight. In that case you are given a provisional boarding pass and you go through passport control to await your fate. If you have a single entry visa and there is no space available then you will not be allowed to leave the departure terminal. In that case, you will have to spend the remainder of your life in the departure terminal, much like the famous film "Terminal" with Tom Hanks.

ABOUT THE AUTHORS

Alexey Goder, Ph.D., is an expert in outsourcing of dual-use technology to overseas countries. He is an innovator and entrepreneur who has been working for over twenty years managing high tech projects in semiconductor, medical and oil exploration industries. The last twelve years have been dedicated to remote managing of offshore engineering teams in the areas where IP protection and export regulation compliance play the most critical role.

Tatiana Gromova holds an MS degree in Optics. She worked as CEO of various outsourcing companies in laser, chemical, solar, semiconductor, and nuclear industries. Tatiana is an expert in jump starting new outsourcing companies from scratch and bringing them to multi-million dollar sustained operations with the focus on customer satisfaction and IP protection.

www.ingramcontent.com/pod-product-compliance
Lightning Source LLC
Chambersburg PA
CBHW051314170526
45166CB00002B/544